US Citizenship Bootcamp

Exercises and Quizzes to Pass

the Naturalization Interview

Jennifer Gagliardi

Host of US Citizenship Podcast

US Citizenship Bootcamp
Exercises and Quizzes to Pass the Naturalization Interview

Printed in the United States of America

ISBN: 978-0998696508

Library of Congress Control Number: 2017935337

ESL Publishing

ESL Publishing is dedicated to producing quality books
for English language learners

www.eslpublishing.com

*This book is dedicated to my parents, Gene and Elinor Gagliardi,
my first teachers in life, love, faith, and freedom.*

TABLE OF CONTENTS

Section 1: Prepare for the English Test

Section 2: Prepare for the Civics Test

Section 3: Appendices & Resources

Introduction

When students prepare for their Citizenship interview, they usually focus on memorizing the 100 Civics and History questions. However, when they go to the interview, they are often surprised that the USCIS (United States Citizenship and Immigration Services) examiner asks 20 to 70 questions from the N-400 Application for Naturalization, and only six to 10 Civics questions, PLUS the students must read and write one sentence in English.

This book is an attempt to help students prepare (or "level-up" as I call it) for their Citizenship interview by presenting 10 interviews based on the N-400, in order of increasing vocabulary and grammatical difficulty.

Please practice the mini-dialogues with a study-buddy. Learn the vocabulary, work on pronunciation, gain fluency, and then move on to the whole interview.

If you have any further questions, concerns, or suggestions, please contact me at uscitizenpod@gmail.com

A Quick Overview of the Naturalization Process

1. Check to see if you are eligible to become a US citizen.
2. Prepare and send in your USCIS N-400 Application for Naturalization.
3. Go to your Fingerprint appointment.
4. Pass your Naturalization Interview.
5. Go to the Oath of Allegiance Ceremony and swear to be a loyal US citizen.

For more information, see these USCIS resources:

- Apply for Citizenship
- B3: I am a permanent resident: How do I apply for US Citizenship?
- B3: Soy residente permanente: ¿Cómo puedo solicitar la ciudadanía estadounidense?
- M-476: A Guide to Naturalization
- M-799: Have You Considered US Citizenship? English/Spanish, Chinese, Korean, Tagalog, Vietnamese
- M-1051: 10 Steps to Naturalization: Understanding the Process of Becoming a US Citizen

Prepare and Submit Your N-400 Application for Naturalization

On April 13, 2016, USCIS revised Form N-400 Application for Naturalization. You must submit an N-400 to become a US citizen. Go to https://www.uscis.gov/n-400 to download the N-400.

- Check the Edition Date (USCIS rejects obsolete forms)
- See where to send in the N-400 (Do you live in the East or West?)
- Determine the Filing Fee for the N-400 (it will go up in 2017)
- Find Special Instructions
- Find Forms for Fee Waiver, or Pay by Credit Card

What happens after I send my N-400?

About two to three weeks after you send in your N-400, you will receive an "N-400 Receipt" letter from the USCIS. On the top of the letter there is a 13-character Receipt Number that begins with three letters (such as EAC, WAC, LIN, or SRC). Use the

Receipt Number to check your case status.

Depending on the local USCIS field office caseload (processing times), you will receive a Fingerprint (biometrics) appointment letter from the USCIS. Go to the USCIS field office at the scheduled place, date, and time. Bring your appointment letter, Green Card, and photo identification. This is a quick appointment to take a digital copy of your fingerprints and a photo. The USCIS will use your biometrics information to run a security (background) check. The USCIS officer *will not* interview you beyond verifying your name and identification.

After the USCIS officer takes your fingerprints and photo, the officer will give you a copy of the M-638 Quick Civics Lessons, which includes a CD of the 100 Civics questions you will need to study. Go home and study! And remember, most of the interview is focused on the N-400. You must also be able to read and write one sentence in English, so use this time wisely.

The Naturalization Interview

After the USCIS completes your background check, you will receive a Citizenship interview appointment letter from the USCIS. Go to the USCIS field office at the scheduled place, date, and time. Bring your appointment letter, Green Card, and photo identification (passport, driver's license, etc.).

Outline of the Naturalization Interview (10 to 15 minutes)

- **Small Talk:** Introduction to the Examiner
- **English Test:** Oral Review of the N-400 (oral response to 20 to 70 questions and commands)
- **Reading Test:** Correctly read one out of three sentences (oral response)
- **Writing Test:** Correctly write one out of three dictated sentences (written response)
- **Civics Test:** Correctly answer six out of 10 questions to the 100 USCIS
- **Civics and History Test** (oral response)

Over 90% of the applicants for US Citizenship pass the Naturalization Interview the first time. Some applicants, however, don't pass one of the tests (usually the N-400 section). If that happens, the USCIS will reschedule the interview one time for free. At the second test, the applicant will be tested only on the section they missed.

The Oath of Allegiance Ceremony

After the applicant passes the interview, he or she will receive an invitation to their Oath of Allegiance Ceremony, during which they will swear allegiance to the United States.

Congratulations! ***You are now a US Citizen!*** You can register to vote and apply for your new US passport!

Section 1

Prepare for the English Test

Outline of the New USCIS N-400

1. **The USCIS N-400:** Download the USCIS N-400 Application for Naturalization from https://www.uscis.gov/n-400. Fill it out. *Do not* fill in your SSN (Social Security Number) on your practice copy. Study the questions, the key vocabulary, and your answers.

2. **USCIS Social Media:** Follow USCIS.gov & USCIS.gov/es on Facebook and Twitter.

3. **The USCIS Citizenship Resource Center**: Try all of the USCIS English and Civics tests resources at https://www.uscis.gov/citizenship/learners/study-test

4. **Flash Cards:** Download the USCIS Civics and English flash cards. Review the Citizenship vocabulary sets on Quizlet.

5. **Videos**: Check out the new USCIS Civics Playlist, which has one video for each question. Follow-up by watching all the videos, and take all the quizzes from Preparing for the Oath. Also look for videos of mock Citizenship interviews on YouTube.

6. **Study-Buddy:** Find a study-buddy. Meet regularly. If you can't meet in person, use Skype or Facetime for 15 minutes every day. Ask each other the N-400 and Civics questions.

7. **Citizenship Class:** Go to a Citizenship class at your local adult school, library, church, or community. If there is no class, start a self-study group. Students learn more by talking and working with each other.

8. **Online Classes via your Library Card:** Ask your local library for access to subscription databases that offer *free* online Citizenship classes *via your library card.* For example, Pronunciator's ProCitizen is similar to SI.edu Preparing for the Oath, and Learning Express has Citizenship Classes in English and Spanish. Be careful: these online classes focus on the Civics questions, and you must also learn about the N-400.

9. **Family Literacy:** Check out age-appropriate books and DVDs from the library about US history and Civics, and read or watch them with your kids. For adult and children's books about the naturalization process, see SCCL's Citizenship Resources.

10. **Family Fun**: Take your kids to National Parks and local historical sites. While visiting the parks, look for Geocaches treasures or Pokémon Go critters. Extend the fun by putting together jigsaw puzzles that feature great American landmarks, such as the Grand Canyon, the Statue of Liberty, or maps of the 50 states.

11. **More English!** If you need more help with your English, check out the resources on USA Learns, VOA Learning English, Cambridge Ventures Arcade, or the Interview Citizenship Resources at the end of this book. Or sign up for an ESL or English conversation class.

Good Luck! I know that you will be a great American Citizen!

Before You Begin: Seven Questions About Exemptions and Accommodations

Vocabulary:

Accommodations
Age
Civics Test

Disability
English Test
Exemption

Impairment
Interpreter
Native Language

Write the correct vocabulary under each picture.

1.	2.	3.
4.	5.	6.
7.	8.	9.

Vocabulary:

Accommodations   Disability   Impairment
Age   English Test   Interpreter
Civics Test   Exemption   Native Language

Write the vocabulary next to the definition.

1. _____: What year were you born? How many years have you lived since your year of birth?
    Example: I was born in 1985. I am 32 years old.

2. _____: A problem that stops a person from moving or understanding.
    Example: I cannot walk and must use a wheelchair.

3. _____: A body part that is weak.
    Example: I am hard-of-hearing. I cannot hear soft voices.

4. _____: The USCIS makes small changes to the interview for some older, longtime residents and disabled people.
    Example: I am deaf and use ASL sign language to communicate.

5. _____: The 100 USCIS History and Government Questions.
    Example: I must answer six out of 10 questions correctly to pass the test.

6. _____: The language that you spoke in your home country.
    Example: I am from China. I can speak Cantonese and Mandarin.

7. _____: The USCIS officer asks questions about your N-400.
    Example: During my interview, I must answer all questions that the USCIS examiner asks me about my N-400 Application for Naturalization.

8. _____: The person who tells another person what someone else says in a different language.
    Example: I cannot hear. I need a person who knows ASL sign language to help me during my Citizenship interview.

9. _____: Some older, longtime residents do not have to do the interview in English.
    Example: People who are age 50 or older <u>and</u> have lived in the US as a Legal Permanent Resident for at least 20 years can do the interview in their native language.

Practice Questions

Practice A: Age

- **How old are you?**
    - I am age (number of years).
    - I am (number) years old.

Practice B: Permanent Residence

- **How many years have you lived in the U.S. as a Legal Permanent Resident?**
    - I have lived in the U.S. as a Legal Permanent Resident for (number years).
    - I have been a Legal Permanent Resident for (number) of years.

Practice C: Native Language

- **What is your native language?**
    - I speak (Arabic / Cantonese / Korean / Mandarin / Spanish / Tagalog / Vietnamese / OTHER: _____).
    - I am from China. My native language is Cantonese. I also speak Mandarin.
    - I am from India. My native languages are Tamil, Hindi, and English. I also speak Telugu and Malayalam.
    - I am from Vietnam. I speak Vietnamese.
    - I am from Somalia. I speak Somali and Arabic.
    - I am from Iran. I speak Farsi and read Arabic.
    - I am from Ethiopia. I speak Amharic, but my mother's family spoke Oromo.
    - I am from Korea. I speak Korean. Although I studied English at school, I didn't speak English until I came to the United States.
    - I am from Mexico. I spoke Nahuatl at home and learned Spanish at school.
    - I am from the Philippines. We speak Tagalog, Ilocano, English, a little Spanish, and some Chinese.

Practice D: English Test

- **Can you read, write, speak, and understand English?**
    - Yes, I can read, write, speak, and understand English.
    - Yes, I can read, write, speak, and understand a little English.
    - No, I cannot read, write, speak, or understand English.

Practice E: Exemption (from the English Test)

- **Are you requesting an exemption from the English test?**
    - No, I am ready to answer the questions about my N-400 Application for Naturalization in English.
    - Yes, I am age 50 or older and have lived in the US as a Legal Permanent Resident for at least 20 years. I request an exemption from the English Test and am ready to answer the N-400 and Civics questions in my native language _____.
    - Yes, I am age 55 or older and have lived in the US as a Legal Permanent Resident for at least 15 years. I request an exemption from the English Test and am ready to answer the N-400 and Civics questions in my native language _____.

Practice F: Civics Test

- **Are you ready to answer six out of 10 Civics questions correctly?**
    - Yes, I am ready.
    - I am age 65 or older and have lived in the US a Legal Permanent Resident for at least 20 years. I can answer six out of 10 questions from the simplified version of the Civics Test.

Accommodation, Disability, Impairment

- **Are you requesting an accommodation to the Naturalization process because of a disability or impairment?**
    - No, I am not requesting an accommodation.
    - Yes, I have a learning disability. I request an exemption from the Civics Test.

- Yes, I have a hearing impairment. I can hear loud voices with my hearing aid. The examiner must speak loudly and clearly.
- Yes, I am deaf. I am requesting an accommodation to bring an ASL interpreter.
- Yes, I use a wheelchair or mobility aid. If the examiner's office is difficult to access, I request an accommodation to have my interview in an office that is easily accessible.
- Yes, I am blind or have low-vision. I request the accommodation to bring my guide dog to the interview. I also request a Braille reading test.
- Yes, I have a disability (describe the disability). Here is my Form N-648, Medical Certification for Disability Exceptions signed by my doctor. I request the following exemption or accommodation (describe the exemption or accommodation).

Seven Questions About Exemptions and Accommodations

1. **How old are you?**
   - I am age (number of years).
   - I am (number) years old.

2. **How many years have you lived in the U.S. as a Legal Permanent Resident?**
   - I have lived in the U.S. as a Legal Permanent Resident for (number of years).

3. **What is your native language?**
   - I speak (Arabic / Cantonese / Korean/ Mandarin / Spanish / Tagalog / Vietnamese / OTHER: _____).

4. **Can you read, write, speak, and understand English?**
   - Yes, I can read, write, speak, and understand English.
   - Yes, I can read, write, speak, and understand a little English.
   - No, I cannot read, write, speak, or understand English.

5. **Are you requesting an exemption from the English test?**
   - No, I am ready to answer the questions about my N-400 Application for Naturalization in English.
   - Yes, I am age 50 or older and have lived in the US as a Legal Permanent Resident for at least 20 years. I request an exemption from the English Test and am ready to answer the N-400 and Civics questions in my native language _____ .
   - Yes, I am age 55 or older and have lived in the US as a Legal Permanent Resident for at least 15 years. I request an exemption from the English Test and am ready to answer the N-400 and Civics questions in my native language _____ .

6. **Are you ready to answer six out of 10 Civics questions correctly?**
   - Yes, I am ready.
   - I am age 65 or older and have lived in the US a Legal Permanent Resident for

at least 20 years. I can answer six out of 10 questions from the simplified version of the civics test.

7. **Are you requesting an accommodation to the Naturalization process because of a disability or impairment?**

   – No, I am not requesting an accommodation.
   – Yes, I am deaf/hard-of-hearing and require an ASL interpreter.
   – Yes, I use a wheelchair or mobility aid.
   – Yes, I am blind. I need to bring my guide dog to the interview.
   – Yes, I have a disability (describe the disability). Here is my Form N-648, Medical Certification for Disability Exceptions signed by my doctor. I request the following exemption or accommodation (describe the exemption or accommodation).

TIP:

For more information about USCIS Accommodations and Exemptions, please go to https://www.uscis.gov/us-citizenship/citizenship-through-naturalization/exceptions-accommodations.

For more information about USCIS Form N-648, Medical Certification for Disability Exceptions, see https://www.uscis.gov/n-648.

Interview 1: Five N-400 Questions and Five Civics Questions

Vocabulary:

Citizen	Name	The Constitution
Married	Permanent Resident	Vote
Month	President	Year

Write the correct vocabulary under each picture.

1.	2.	3.

4.	5.	6.

7.	8.	9.

Vocabulary:

Citizen	Name	The Constitution
Married	Permanent Resident	Vote
Month	President	Year

Write the vocabulary next to the definition.

1. _____: 365 days or 12 months.
   Example: I came to the United States in 2012 and have been a Legal Permanent Resident for 5 years.

2. _____: One of the 12 parts of the year. Most months have 30 or 31 days. February has 28 or 29 days.
   Example: We vote for the President in November.

3. _____: The highest law in the United States.
   Example: The Constitution is the supreme law of the land.

4. _____: To choose a leader or law.
   Example: We vote for the President every four years.

5. _____: The leader of the United States.
   Example: The President is the leader of the United States.

6. _____: The words people use to call or talk about you.
   Example: In China, people called me Chen Fu-Chiu. My family name is Chen. My given name is Fu-Chiu. In the United States, people call me Fu-Chiu Chen. My first name is Fu-Chiu. I don't have a middle name. My last name is Chen.

7. _____: To be someone's husband or wife according to the law.
   Example: I have been married to my husband for three years.

8. _____: A person who is not a US citizen that the US government says can live in the United States.
   Example: I am a Legal Permanent Resident. I have lived in the US since 2012.

9. _____: A person who was born in a country or became a member through the law (naturalization).
   Example: My husband is a citizen. We have been married for 3 years. I have been a permanent resident for 3 years. Now I am studying to become a citizen.

Practice Questions

Practice A: Name

- **What is your name?**
  - (First name / Last name)

- **What is the name of the current President of the United States?**
  - Donald Trump

Practice B: Permanent Resident

- **Are you a Legal Permanent Resident?**
  - Yes

- **How many years have you been a permanent resident?**
  - (Number) years

- **We elect a President for how many years?**
  - Four (4) years

Practice C: Married to a US Citizen

- **Are you married to a US citizen?**
  - Yes
  - No

- **In what month do we vote for President?**
  - November

Practice D: US Constitution

- **Do you support the US Constitution?**
  - Yes

- **What is the supreme law of the land?**
  - The Constitution

Five N-400 Questions and Five Civics Questions

N-400 Questions

1. **What is your name?**

   – My name is (first name / last name).

2. **Are you a Legal Permanent Resident?**

   – Yes, I am a Legal Permanent Resident.

3. **How many years have you been a permanent resident?**

   – I have been a Legal Permanent Resident for (number) years.

4. **Are you married to a US citizen?**

   – Yes, I am married to a US citizen.
   – No, I am not married to a US citizen.

5. **Do you support the US Constitution?**

   – Yes, I support the US Constitution.

Civics Questions

1. **What is the name of the current President of the United States?**

   – Answer:_____

2. **We elect a President for how many years?**

   – Answer:_____

3. **In what month do we vote for President?**

   – Answer:_____

4. **What is the supreme law of the land?**

   – Answer:_____

5. **What does the Constitution do?**

— Answer:_____

Interview 2: Ten N-400 Questions and Five Civics Questions

Vocabulary:

Address	Country of Birth	State Capital
Arrested	Date of Birth	US Capital
Children	Independence Day	Work

Write the correct vocabulary under each picture.

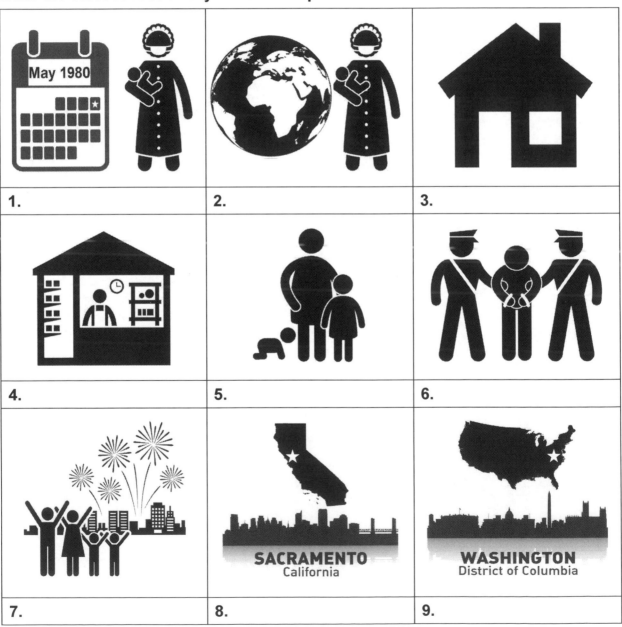

1.

2.

3.

4.

5.

6.

7.

8.

9.

Vocabulary:

Address	Country of Birth	State Capital
Arrested	Date of Birth	US Capital
Children	Independence Day	Work

Write the vocabulary next to the definition.

1. _____ : A job that I am paid to do.
   Example: I am a cashier at a fast food restaurant.

2. _____ : The country where I was born.
   Example: I was born in Vietnam.

3. _____ : The date when I was born (month / day / year).
   Example: I was born on October 5, 1973.

4. _____ : My son, daughter, or a dependent that I adopted before his
   or her 18th birthday.
   Example: I have a daughter and a baby boy.

5. _____ : The city where a state's government meets.
   Example: The capital of California is Sacramento.

6. _____ : The city where the federal government meets.
   Example: The capital of the United States is Washington, D.C.

7. _____ : The day every year on which the United States celebrates
   its freedom from Great Britain (July 4, 1776).
   Example: My city has a fireworks show every year on the Fourth of July.

8. _____ : Location information about the place where I live or work.
   Example: house number / street name / apartment number / city / state / zip code
   Example: I live at 1331 E. Calaveras Blvd. #407, Milpitas, CA 95035
   Example: Company name / street name and number / city / state / zip code
   Example: I work at SanDisk, 951 Technology Dr. #400, Milpitas, CA 95035

9. _____ : To break the law and go to jail.
   Example: I took a new phone without paying for it. The store manager stopped
   me and called the police. The police took me to jail.

Practice Questions

Practice A: Full Name

- **What is your first name?**

  – My first name is (first name).

- **What is your middle name?**

  – My middle name is (middle name).

- **What is your last name?**

  – My last name is (last name).

- **Spell your last name.**

  – (Spell your l-a-s-t-n-a-m-e)

- **What is your full name?**

  – My full name is (first name / middle name / last name)

- **Name two national US holidays.**

  – Martin Luther King, Jr. Day and Independence Day

Practice B: Date and Country of Birth

- **What is your date of birth?**

  – My date of birth is (month / day/ year).

- **What is your country of birth?**

  – My country of birth is (name of country).

- **When do we celebrate Independence Day?**

  – July 4

Practice C: Home Address, Work, Travel

- **What is your address?**
    - My address is (street number / street name / city / state / zip code).

- **Do you work?**
    - Yes, I do.
    - No, I don't.

- **Have you traveled outside of the US?**
    - Yes, I have.
    - No, I haven't.

- **Name one state that borders Mexico.**
    - California

Practice D: Marital Status, Children

- **Are you married?**
    - Yes, I am.
    - No, I'm not.

- **Do you have children?**
    - Yes, I do.
    - No, I don't.

- **What is the capital of your state?**
    - Sacramento is the capital of California.
    - My state capital is (see List of State Capitals at https://simple.wikipedia.org/wiki/List_of_U.S._states).

Practice E: Part 12—Additional Information

- **Have you ever been arrested?**

    – No, I haven't.

- **Do you support the Constitution?**

    – Yes, I do.

- **What is the capital of the United States?**

    – Washington, D.C.

Ten N-400 Questions and Five Civics Questions

N-400 Questions

1. What is your full name?

- My full name is (first name / middle name / last name).

2. What is your date of birth?

- My date of birth is (month / day / year).

3. What is your country of birth?

- My country of birth is (name of country).

4. What is your address?

- My address is (street number / street name / city / state / zip code).

5. Do you work?

- Yes, I work.
- No, I don't work.

6. Have you traveled outside of the US?

- Yes, I have traveled outside of the US.
- No, I have never traveled outside of the US.

7. Are you married?

- Yes, I am married.
- No, I'm not married.

8. Do you have children?

- I don't have any children.
- I have one child.
- I have (number) children.

9. **Have you ever been arrested?**

   – No, I have never been arrested.

10. **Do you support the Constitution?**

   – Yes, I support the US Constitution.

Civics Questions

1. **Name two national US holidays.**

   – Answer:_____

2. **When do we celebrate Independence Day?**

   – Answer:_____

3. **Name one state that borders Mexico.**

   – Answer:_____

4. **What is the capital of your state?**

   – Answer:_____

5. **What is the capital of the United States?**

   – Answer:_____

Interview 3: Fifteen N-400 Questions and Six Civics Questions

Vocabulary:

Claim	Marital Status	Taxes
Divorced	Single	Truth
Law	Statue of Liberty	Widowed

Write the correct vocabulary under each picture.

1.	2.	3.
4.	5.	6.
7.	8.	9.

Vocabulary:

Claim	Marital Status	Taxes
Divorced	Single	Truth
Law	Statue of Liberty	Widowed

Write the vocabulary next to the definition.

1. _____: An important symbol of freedom. It is on Liberty Island in New York Harbor.
   Example: This statue welcomes immigrants to America.

2. _____: Are you single, married, widowed, or divorced?
   Example: I am not single. I have been married three times. My first marriage ended in divorce. I got married again, but I was widowed when my second wife died. I got married for a third time, and I very happy with my new wife.

3. _____: Money to pay for the government, military, healthcare, schools, etc.
   Example: April 15 is the last day to send your Form 1040 to the IRS.

4. _____: A person who has never been married.
   Example: I have never been married.

5. _____: The spouse who is still alive after the other spouse dies.
   Example: I got married in 2002 and my spouse died in 2010.

6. _____: The system of rules that the people must follow.
   Example: I am a Legal Permanent Resident. I follow the rules to live in the United States.

7. _____: To legally end a marriage.
   Example: I got married in 2002 and ended the marriage in 2009.

8. _____: To say something true that is supported by facts.
   Example: I am a Legal Permanent Resident. I can prove this by showing you my Legal Permanent Resident Card. I promise that everything that I say during my Citizenship interview is true.

9. _____: To lie or say something false that is not supported by facts.
   Example: I have never lied and said that I was a US citizen. I cannot prove that I am a US because I only have a Legal Permanent Resident Card and don't have a certificate of naturalization.

Practice Questions

Practice A: Immigration Status

- **What is your immigration status?**
  - I am a Legal Permanent Resident.

- **When did you become a Legal Permanent Resident?**
  - (month / day/ year)

- **What is one reason colonists came to America?**
  - Freedom

Practice B: Home Address, Work, Travel

- **Where do you live?**
  - My address is (street number / street name / city / state / zip code).

- **How do you support yourself?**
  - I work.
  - I go to school.
  - My (husband / wife / family) supports me.

- **Have you taken any trips outside of the US?**
  - Yes, I have.
  - No, I haven't.

- **Where is the Statue of Liberty?**
  - New York Harbor

Practice C: Marital Status

- **What is your marital status?**
  - I am single.

- I am married.
- I am widowed.
- I am divorced.

- **Name one branch or part of the government.**
  - Congress

Practice D: Claim

- **Have you ever claimed to be a US citizen?**
  - No, I haven't.

- **Name one right only for United States citizens.**
  - To vote in a federal election.

Practice E: Taxes

- **Do you pay your taxes every year?**
  - Yes, I pay my taxes.
  - No, I don't pay taxes.

- **When is the last day you can send in federal income tax forms?**
  - April 15

Practice F: Arrested

- **Have you ever been arrested?**
  - No, I haven't.
  - Yes, I have.

- **What is the "rule of law"?**
  - Everyone must follow the law.

Fifteen N-400 Questions and Six Civics Questions

N-400 Questions

1. **What is your immigration status?**

   – I am a Legal Permanent Resident.

2. **When did you become a Legal Permanent Resident?**

   – I became a Legal Permanent Resident on (month / day / year).

3. **What is your full name?**

   – My name is (first name / middle name / last name).

4. **When were you born?**

   – I was born on (month/day/year).

5. **Where were you born?**

   – I was born in (name of country).

6. **Where do you live?**

   – I live at (street number / street name / city / state / zip code).

7. **How do you support yourself?**

   – I work.
   – I go to school.
   – My (husband / wife / family) supports me.

8. **Have you taken any trips outside of the US?**

   – Yes, I have taken (number) trips outside of the US.
   – No, I have never taken any trips outside of the US.

9. **What is your marital status?**

   – I am single.
   – I am married.

- I am widowed.
- I am divorced.

10. Do you have any children?

- I have one child.
- I have (number) children.
- I don't have any children.

11. Have you ever claimed to be a US citizen?

- No, I have never claimed to be a US citizen.

12. Do you pay your taxes every year?

- Yes, I pay my taxes every year.

13. Have you ever been arrested or committed a crime?

- No, I have never been arrested or committed a crime.

14. Do you support the Constitution?

- Yes, I support the US Constitution.

15. Do you promise that everything you said was true?

- Yes, everything that I said was true.

Civics Questions

1. What is one reason colonists came to America?

- Answer:_____

2. Where is the Statue of Liberty?

- Answer:_____

3. Name one branch or part of the government.

- Answer:_____

4.   **Name one right only for United States citizens.**

        – Answer:_____

5.   **When is the last day you can send in federal income tax forms?**

        – Answer:_____

6.   **What is the "rule of law"?**

        – Answer:_____

Interview 4: Twenty N-400 Questions and Six Civics Questions

Vocabulary:

Congress	Hurt	Resident 5 years
Crime	Resident/Married 3 years	Territory
Eligibility	Previous Address	War

Write the correct vocabulary under each picture.

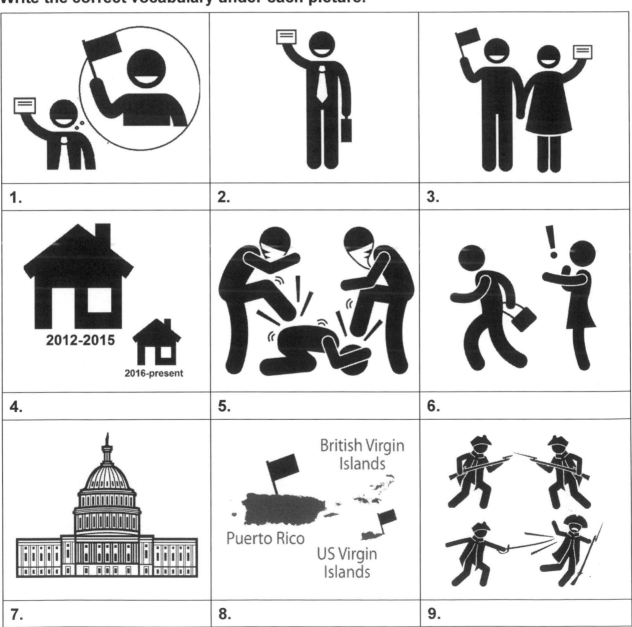

1.

2.

3.

4.

5.

6.

7.

8.

9.

Vocabulary:

Congress	Hurt	Resident 5 years
Crime	Resident/Married 3 years	Territory
Eligibility	Previous Address	War

Write the vocabulary next to the definition.

1. _____: Also known as the Legislative Branch. It is the part of the US government that makes federal laws.
    Example: Lawmakers meet in the Capitol Building in Washington, D.C.

2. _____: Armies fight against each other.
    Example: The American colonists fought the British because of high taxes.

3. _____: Land that is owned or controlled by a federal government.
    Example: The United States governs two groups of islands in the Caribbean: Puerto Rico and the US Virgin Islands.

4. _____: The law says that you have met the legal requirements to do something, such as become US citizen.
    Example: Are you eligible to become a US citizen? Go to https://goo.gl/Uuiuj5

5. _____: The place where you lived before your current home.
    Example: From 2012-2015, I lived in San Jose. Now I live in Milpitas.

6. _____: To attack and injure a person on purpose.
    Example: I have never planned to hurt or kill a person.

7. _____: To be eligible to become a US citizen based on 3 years of permanent residence plus marriage to a US citizen, who has been a citizen for 3 years.
    Example: I have been married to a US citizen for 3 years. I have been a Legal Permanent Resident for 3 years and have lived in the US for 3 years.

8. _____: To be eligible to become a US citizen based on 5 years of permanent residence.
    Example: Although I have lived in the United States for 25 years, I have been a Legal Permanent Resident for only 5 years. I can now apply for US Citizenship.

9. _____: To break the law such as stealing or selling illegal drugs.
    Example: I stole a purse. I used the cash to buy illegal drugs. Then I sold the drugs and was arrested by the police. I broke the law and went to jail.

Practice Questions

Practice A: Eligibility

- **How are you eligible to become a US Citizen?**
  - I have been a US Legal Permanent Resident for 5 years.
  - I have been a US Legal Permanent Resident for 3 years and married to a US citizen for 3 years.

- **What are the two parts of the US Congress?**
  - The Senate and House (of Representatives)

Practice B: Current and Previous Home Address

- **What is your phone number?**
  - My phone number is (area code and phone number).

- **What is your current home address?**
  - (house number / street name / apartment number / city / state / zip code)

- **When did you move to your current home address?**
  - (month / day / year)

- **What is your previous home address?**
  - (house number / street name / apartment number / city / state / zip code)

- **When did you live at your previous home address?**
  - I lived at my old home from (month / day / year) to (month / day / year).

- **Name one US territory.**
  - Puerto Rico

Practice C: Claimed and Vote

- **Have you ever claimed to be a US citizen?**
  - No

- **Have you ever registered to vote in a US election?**
  - No

- **Have you ever voted in any US elections?**
  - No

- **What is one responsibility that is only for United States citizens?**
  - To vote in a federal election.

Practice D: Taxes

- **Do you pay your taxes every year?**
  - Yes
  - No, I have no income.

- **Do you owe any overdue taxes?**
  - No

- **Why did the colonists fight the British?**
  - Because of high taxes (taxation without representation).

Practice E: Crime

- **Have you ever badly hurt or killed a person on purpose?**
  - No

- **Have you ever been arrested or committed a crime?**
  - No

- **Name one war fought by the United States in the 1800s.**
  - The Civil War

Practice F: Attachment to the Constitution

- **Do you support the Constitution?**
  - Yes

- **The idea of self-government is in the first three words of the Constitution. What are these words?**
  - We the People

Twenty N-400 Questions and Six Civics Questions

N-400 Questions

1. **How are you eligible to become a US Citizen?**

    - I have been a US Legal Permanent Resident for 5 years.
    - I have been a US Legal Permanent Resident for 3 years and married to a US citizen for 3 years.

2. **What is your current legal name?**

    - My current legal name is (first name / middle name / last name).

3. **What is your phone number?**

    - My phone number is (area code) (phone number).

4. **What is your current home address?**

    - My current home address is (house number / street name / (apartment number) / city / state / zip code).

5. **When did you move to your current home address?**

    - I moved to my current home address (month / day / year).

6. **What is your previous home address?**

    - My previous home address was (house number / street name / apartment number / city / state / zip code).

7. **When did you live at your previous home address?**

    - I lived at my previous home address from (month/day/year) to (month/day/year).

8. **Do you work?**

    - I work.
    - I go to school.
    - I stay at home and take care of my family.
    - I am retired.

9. **Have you taken any trips outside of the US?**

    – Yes, I left the US on (month / day / year) and returned (month / day / year).

    – No, I have not left the US

10. **What is your marital status?**

    – I am single.

    – I am married.

    – I am widowed.

    – I am divorced.

11. **Do you have children?**

    – I have one child.

    – I have (number) children.

    – I don't have any children.

12. **Have you ever claimed to be a US citizen?**

    – No, I have never claimed to be a US citizen.

13. **Have you ever registered to vote in a US election?**

    – No, I have never registered to vote in a US election.

14. **Have you ever voted in any US elections?**

    – No, I have never voted in a US election.

15. **Do you pay your taxes every year?**

    – Yes, I pay my taxes ever year.

    – No, I have no income.

16. **Do you owe any overdue taxes?**

    – No, I don't owe any overdue taxes.

    – Yes, I owe some overdue taxes.

17. **Have you ever badly hurt or killed a person on purpose?**

    – No, I have never hurt or killed anyone.

18. **Have you ever been arrested or committed a crime?**

    – No, I have never been arrested or committed a crime.

19. **Do you support the Constitution?**

    – Yes. I support the Constitution.

20. **Do you promise that everything on your N-400 is true?**

    – Yes, I promise that everything I said is true.

Civics Questions

1. **What are the two parts of the US Congress?**

    – Answer:_____

2. **Name one US territory.**

    – Answer:_____

3. **What is one responsibility that is only for United States citizens?**

    – Answer:_____

4. **Why did the colonists fight the British?**

    – Answer:_____

5. **Name one war fought by the United States in the 1800s.**

    – Answer:_____

6. **The idea of self-government is in the first three words of the Constitution. What are these words?**

    – Answer:_____

Interview 5: Twenty-Five N-400 Questions and Six Civics Questions

Vocabulary:

Country of Nationality	Form of Government	Legal Name
Driver's License	George Washington	River
Economic System	Green Card	Travel

Write the correct vocabulary under each picture.

1.

2.

3.

4.

5.

6.

7.

8.

9.

Vocabulary:

Country of Nationality   Form of Government   Legal Name
Driver's License   George Washington   River
Economic System   Green Card   Travel

Write the vocabulary next to the definition:

1. _____: A common name for a Legal Permanent Resident Card.
   Example: My legal name is different from the name on my Legal Permanent Resident Card because I got married.

2. _____: A large body of water that flows across a country.
   Example: The Mississippi flows south from Minnesota to the Gulf of Mexico.

3. _____: My legal first, middle, and last names in the United States.
   Example: In Mexico, my given name is Maria; my middle name is Guadalupe; my father's family name is Rios and my mother's family name is Sanchez. In the United States, my legal name is Maria Guadalupe Garcia. My first name is Maria and my middle name is Guadalupe. When I got married, I changed my last name to my husband's family name, Garcia. Everyone calls me by my nickname, Lupe.

4. _____: State-issued identification which permits me to drive.
   Example: States have the power to give driver's licenses to their residents.

5. _____: The country of which I am currently a citizen.
   Example: I was born in Hong Kong and am a citizen of Canada.

6. _____: The first President of the United States.
   Example: Americans call their first President the "Father of the Country."

7. _____: The system of government.
   Example: The US is a democracy: people vote for their leaders.

8. _____: The way a country makes, manages, and spends money.
   Example: An American business owner runs a business to make money (profit). After the owner pays the workers, expenses, and debts, the owner can keep or reinvest the profit in the business.

9. _____: To go outside of the United States for more than 24 hours.
   Example: I go to Mexico every year for three weeks to visit my family. On my most recent trip, I left on December 15, 2016 and returned January 7, 2017.

Practice Questions

Practice A: Eligibility

- **Tell me how you are eligible to become a US Citizen.**

  - I am over 18 years old and I have been a Legal Permanent Resident for 5 years.
  - I am over 18 years old and I have been a Legal Permanent Resident for 3 years, and married to a US citizen for 3 years.

- **How many US Senators are there?**

  - One hundred (100)

Practice B: Legal Name

- **What is your current legal name?**

  - My current legal name is (first name / middle name / last name).

- **Is your legal name the same as the name on your Green Card?**

  - Yes, it is.
  - No, it isn't.

- **Under our Constitution, some powers belong to the states. What is one power of the states?**

  - Give a driver's license.

Practice C: Origins

- **What is your date of birth?**

  - My date of birth is (month / day / year).

- **What is your date of permanent residence?**

  - My date of permanent residence is (month / day / year).

- **What is your country of birth?**
  - My country of birth is (name of country).

- **What is your country of nationality?**
  - My country of nationality is (name of country).

- **Was your mother or father a US citizen before you were 18 years old?**
  - No, they were not.
  - My father was a US citizen before I was 18 years old.
  - My mother was a US citizen before I was 18 years old.

- **Who is the "Father of Our Country"?**
  - (George) Washington

Practice D: Travel

- **Have you taken on any trips outside of the US?**
  - I took one trip.
  - I took (number) trips.
  - I have not taken any trips.

- **How many total days were you outside of the US?**
  - I was outside the US for (number) days.
  - I was never outside of the US.

- **What date did you leave and what date did you return?**
  - I left on (month / day / year) and returned on (month / day / year).

- **Name one of the two longest rivers in the United States.**
  - Mississippi River

Practice E: Claim, Vote, Taxes, Crime, Deported

- **Have you ever claimed to be a US citizen?**
  - No, never.

- **Have you ever voted in any US elections?**
  - No, never.

- **Do you pay your taxes every year?**
  - Yes, I pay my taxes ever year.
  - No, I don't pay taxes. I don't have any income.

- **Have you ever been a terrorist or done anything violent?**
  - No, never.

- **Have you ever been arrested or committed a crime?**
  - No, never.

- **Have you ever been deported?**
  - No, never.

- **What is the economic system in the United States?**
  - Capitalist economy

Practice F: Attachment to the Constitution

- **Do you support the Constitution and the US form of government?**
  - Yes

- **Are you willing to bear arms in the US armed forces?**
  - Yes

- **Are you willing to perform noncombatant services for the US armed forces?**

  – Yes

- **Are you willing to help the government during a national emergency?**

  – Yes

- **What is one promise you make when you become a United States citizen?**

  – Give up loyalty to other countries.

Twenty-Five N-400 Questions and Six Civics Questions

N-400 Questions

1. **Tell me how you are eligible to become a US Citizen.**

   - I am over 18 years old and I have been a Legal Permanent Resident for 5 years.
   - I am over 18 years old and I have been a Legal Permanent Resident for 3 years, and married to a US citizen for 3 years.

2. **What is your current legal name?**

   - My current legal name is (first name / middle name / last name).

3. **Is your legal name the same as the name on your Green Card?**

   - Yes, it is.
   - No, it isn't. I got married and changed my last name.

4. **What is your date of birth?**

   - My date of birth is (month / day / year).

5. **What is your date of permanent residence?**

   - My date of permanent residence is (month / day / year).

6. **What is your country of birth?**

   - My country of birth is (name of country).

7. **What is your country of nationality?**

   - My country of nationality is (name of country).

8. **What is your current home address?**

   - My current home address is (house number / street name / apartment number / city / state / zip code).

9. **Was your mother or father a US citizen before you were 18 years old?**

- No, they were not.
- My father was a US citizen before I was 18 years old.
- My mother was a US citizen before I was 18 years old.

10. **Do you work or go to school?**

- Yes, I work.
- Yes, I go to school.
- I stay at home and take care of my family.
- I am retired.

11. **Have you taken on any trips outside of the US?**

- Yes, I took one trip outside of the US.
- Yes, I took (number) trips outside of the US.
- No, I have not taken any trips outside of the US.

12. **How many total days were you outside of the US?**

- I was outside the US for a total of (number) days.
- I was never outside of the US.

13. **What date did you leave and what date did you return?**

- I left on (month / day / year) and returned on (month / day / year).

14. **What is your marital status?**

- I am single.
- I am married.
- I am widowed.
- I am divorced.

15. **Do you have any children?**

- I have one child.
- I have (number) children.
- I don't have any children.

16. **Have you ever claimed to be a US citizen?**

  – No, I have never claimed to be a US citizen.

17. **Have you ever voted in any US elections?**

  – No, I have never voted in any US elections.

18. **Do you pay your taxes every year?**

  – Yes, I pay my taxes ever year.
  – No, I don't pay taxes because I have no income.

19. **Have you ever been a terrorist or done anything violent?**

  – No, I have never been a terrorist or done anything violent.

20. **Have you ever been arrested or committed a crime?**

  – No, I have never been arrested or done anything violent.

21. **Have you ever been deported?**

  – No, I have never been deported.

22. **Do you support the Constitution and the US form of government?**

  – Yes, I support the Constitution and the US form or government.

23. **Are you willing to bear arms in the US armed forces?**

  – Yes, I am willing to bear arms in the US armed forces.

24. **Are you willing to perform noncombatant services for the US armed forces?**

  – Yes, I am willing to perform noncombatant services for the US armed forces.

25. **Are you willing to help the government during a national emergency?**

  – Yes, I am willing to help the government during a national emergency.

Civics Questions

1. **How many US Senators are there?**

    – Answer:_____

2. **Under our Constitution, some powers belong to the states. What is one power of the states?**

    – Answer:_____

3. **Who is the "Father of Our Country"?**

    – Answer:_____

4. **Name one of the two longest rivers in the United States.**

    – Answer:_____

5. **What is the economic system in the United States?**

    – Answer:_____

6. **What is one promise you make when you become a United States citizen?**

    – Answer:_____

Interview 6: Thirty N-400 Questions and Seven Civics Questions

Vocabulary:

Amendment
Bear Arms
Deported

Emergency
Native American
Nobility

Noncombatant
Senator
Terrorist

Write the correct vocabulary under each picture.

1.

2.

3.

4.

5.

6.

7.

8.

9.

Vocabulary:

Amendment	Emergency	Noncombatant
Bear Arms	Native American	Senator
Deported	Nobility	Terrorist

Write the vocabulary next to the definition.

1. _____: A big problem that can hurt or kill many people, such as an earthquake, flood, or tornado.
   Example: After the earthquake, we helped give food and water to the people who lost their homes.

2. _____: A change or addition to the Constitution.
   Example: In 1791, the Bill of Rights was added the Constitution. The Bill of Rights lists the basic rights of all Americans.

3. _____: A member of a king or queen's royal family.
   Example: We do not have a royal family in the US. If a person has a title of nobility in their country, he or she must renounce it before they become a US citizen.

4. _____: People who use violence to destroy governments.
   Example: On September 11, 2001, al-Qaeda crashed planes into the World Trade Center and the Pentagon to create fear and chaos in America.

5. _____: The people who are the original residents of the Americas.
   Example: The Cherokee originally lived in what is now known as Alabama, Georgia, and the Carolinas, and now live in Oklahoma.

6. _____: A person who represents a state in the US Senate.
   Example: People elected to the US Senate serve for six years.

7. _____: To be arrested and sent back to my old country.
   Example: I overstayed my visa. I was arrested for stealing and selling drugs. I was sent back to my home country.

8. _____: To use a weapon to protect the country.
   Example: Jose is a soldier in the US Army. He carries a gun on duty.

9. _____: To work in the US armed forces without using weapons.
   Example: Anna is a doctor in the US Army. She does not use a gun on duty. She takes care of sick and injured people.

Practice Questions

Practice A: Claim

- **Have you ever claimed to be a US citizen?**

  – No, never.

- **What is "to claim"?**

  – A non-citizen lies and says: "I am a US citizen."

- **What is an amendment?**

  – A change (to the Constitution).

Practice B: Vote

- **Have you ever voted in any US elections?**

  – No, never.

- **What is to "vote"?**

  – A citizen chooses a new leader or law.

- **We elect a US Senator for how many years?**

  – Six (6).

Practice C: Taxes

- **Do you pay your income taxes every year?**
  – Yes, I do.
  – No, I don't because I have no income.

- **What is "income tax"?**

  – Income tax is to pay money to the government based on what I earn.

- **Under our Constitution, some powers belong to the federal government. What is one power of the federal government?**
  - To print money.

Practice D: Terrorism

- **Have you ever been a terrorist or done anything violent?**
  - No, never.

- **What is "terrorism"?**
  - A terrorist uses violence to control people and governments.

- **What major event happened on September 11, 2001, in the United States?**
  - Terrorists attacked the United States.

Practice E: Crime

- **Have you ever been arrested or committed a crime?**
  - No, never.
  - Yes, I was arrested (month / day / year) at (city / state) for (name of the crime). Here are my court records.

- **What is "crime"?**
  - Crime is to break the law, for example: to steal, or sell illegal drugs.

- **Who lived in America before the Europeans arrived?**
  - American Indians

Practice F: Deported

- **Have you ever been deported?**
  - No, never.

- **What is "deported"?**
  - Deported is to be arrested and sent back to my old country.

- **What territory did the United States buy from France in 1803?**
  - The Louisiana Territory

Practice G: Bear Arms, Noncombatant, National Emergency

- **If the law requires it, are you willing to bear arms in the US armed forces?**
  - Yes

- **If the law requires it, are you willing to perform noncombatant services for the US armed forces?**
  - Yes

- **If the law requires it, are you willing to help the government during a national emergency?**
  - Yes

- **What is one promise you make when you become a United States citizen?**
  - Defend the Constitution and laws of the United States.

Thirty N-400 Questions and Seven Civics Questions

N-400 Questions

1. **Tell me how you are eligible to become a US Citizen.**

   - I am over 18 years old and I have been a Legal Permanent Resident for 5 years.
   - I am over 18 years old and I have been a Legal Permanent Resident for 3 years, and married to a US citizen for 3 years.

2. **Is your legal name the same as the name on your Green Card?**

   - Yes, it is.
   - No, it isn't. I got married and changed my last name.
   - No, it isn't. I got divorced and changed my last name.
   - No, it isn't. I went to court and changed my name.

3. **What is your date of birth?**

   - My date of birth is (month / day / year).

4. **What is your date of permanent residence?**

   - My date of permanent residence is (month / day / year).

5. **What is your country of birth?**

   - My country of birth is (name of country).

6. **What is your country of nationality?**

   - My country of nationality is (name of country).

7. **What is your current home address?**

   - My current home address is (house number / street name / apartment number / city / state / zip code).

8.   **Do you work or go to school?**

   – I work at (company name).
   – I go to school at (school name).
   – My spouse works at (company name).
   – I am retired. I get a pension.

9.   **Have you taken any trips outside of the US?**

   – Yes, I took one trip outside of the US.
   – Yes, I took (number) trips outside of the US.
   – No, I have not taken any trips outside of the US.

10.   **What date did you leave and what date did you return?**

   – I left on (month / day / year) and returned on (month / day / year).

11.   **What is your marital status?**

   – I am single.
   – I am married.
   – I am widowed.
   – I am divorced.

12.   **Do you have any children?**

   – I have one child.
   – I have (number) children.
   – I don't have any children.

13.   **Have you ever claimed to be a US citizen?**

   – No, I have never claimed to be a US citizen.

14.   **What is "claim"?**

   – A non-citizen lies and says: "I am a US citizen."

15.   **Have you ever voted in any US elections?**

   – No, I have never voted in any US elections.

16. **What is "vote"?**

    – A citizen chooses a new leader or law.

17. **Do you have any title of nobility in a foreign country?**

    – No, I don't have any title of nobility in another country.

18. **What is "nobility"?**

    – Nobility is to be a member of the family of a king or queen.

19. **Do you pay your income taxes every year?**

    – Yes, I pay my income taxes ever year.

    – No, I don't pay taxes because I have no income.

20. **What is "income tax"?**

    – Income tax is to pay money to the government based on what I earn.

21. **Have you ever been a terrorist or done anything violent?**

    – No, I have never been a terrorist or done anything violent.

22. **What is "terrorism"?**

    – A terrorist uses violence to control people and governments.

23. **Have you ever been arrested or committed a crime?**

    – No, I have never been arrested or committed a crime.

    – Yes, I was arrested (month / day / year) at (city / state) for (name of the crime). Here are my court records.

24. **What is "crime"?**

    – Crime is to break the law, for example: to steal, or sell illegal drugs.

25. **Have you ever been deported?**

    – No, I have never been deported.

26. **What is "deported"?**

    – Deported is to be arrested and sent back to my old country.

27.   **Do you support the Constitution and the US form of government?**

  −   Yes, I support the Constitution and the US form or government.

28.   **If the law requires it, are you willing to bear arms in the US armed forces?**

  −   Yes, I am willing to bear arms in the US armed forces.

29.   **If the law requires it, are you willing to perform noncombatant services for the US armed forces?**

  −   Yes, I am willing to perform noncombatant services for the US armed forces.

30.   **If the law requires it, are you willing to help the government during a national emergency?**

  −   Yes, I am willing to help the government during a national emergency.

Civics Questions

1.   **What is an amendment?**

  −   Answer:_____

2.   **We elect a US Senator for how many years?**

  −   Answer:_____

3.   **Under our Constitution, some powers belong to the federal government. What is one power of the federal government?**

  −   Answer:_____

4.   **What major event happened on September 11, 2001, in the United States?**

  −   Answer:_____

5.   **Who lived in America before the Europeans arrived?**

  −   Answer:_____

6.   **What territory did the United States buy from France in 1803?**

  −   Answer:_____

7. **What is one promise you make when you become a United States citizen?**

— Answer:_____

Interview 7: Thirty-Five N-400 Questions and Eight Civics Questions

Vocabulary:

Cabinet	Illegal Drugs	Legally Incompetent
Communism	Illegal Gambling	Port of Entry
Habitual Drunkard	Judicial Branch	Declaration of Independence

Write the correct vocabulary under each picture.

1.

2.

3.

4.

5.

6.

7.

8.

9.

Vocabulary:

Cabinet   Illegal Drugs   Legally Incompetent
Communism   Illegal Gambling   Port of Entry
Habitual Drunkard   Judicial Branch   Declaration of Independence

Write the vocabulary next to the definition.

1. _____: A person who is addicted to alcohol.
   Example: A habitual drunkard drinks too much alcohol every day and gets sick.

2. _____: A person who cannot make his or her own decisions.
   Example: A doctor said that I am too sick to understand anything. A judge appointed my sister to be my legal guardian and make decisions for me.

3. _____: A political party that supports a state-planned economy.
   Example: The government parties of China, Vietnam, North Korea, and Cuba control their economic systems.

4. _____: An announcement that said that the US is a free country.
   Example: Jefferson wrote that all people are created equal and must have life and liberty to pursue happiness.

5. _____: Drugs that are against the law.
   Example: I have never sold or smuggled heroin, opium, or cocaine.

6. _____: The group of federal department leaders (secretaries) that advise the President.
   Example: The Secretary of Commerce and the Secretary of Labor advise the President on business and workers' rights.

7. _____: The part of government that reviews and explains laws.
   Example: The Supreme Court is the highest court in the US. It decides if a law goes against the Constitution.

8. _____: The place where a person can legally enter a country.
   Example: I visited the US many times. When I came live here, I went through Customs at the San Francisco Airport (SFO).

9. _____: To play cards or games for money and not pay taxes.
   Example: I like to go to casinos. If I win, I pay taxes on my winnings.

Practice Questions

Practice A: Country and Port of Entry

- **What is your country of birth?**

  - (name of country)

- **What is your country of nationality?**

  - (name of country)

- **What was your port of entry?**

  - My port of entry was (airport or border crossing where you entered the US).

- **Name one state that borders Canada.**

  - Alaska

Practice B: Work

- **What do you do for a living?**

  - I work.
  - I go to school.
  - My spouse works.
  - My family supports me.
  - I am retired. I get a pension.
  - I am retired. I get a Social Security check.
  - I am disabled. I get a Social Security check.
  - I am unemployed. I get Unemployment.

- **What are two cabinet-level positions?**

  - Secretary of Health and Human Services
  - Secretary of Labor

Practice C: Trips Outside of the US

- **Have you taken any trips outside of the US?**
    - Yes, I took one trip outside of the US.
    - Yes, I took (number) trips outside of the US. (Go to the next section.)
    - No, I have not taken any trips outside of the US.

- **How many total days were you outside of the US?**
    - I was outside the US for (number) days.

- **Tell me about your last trip: when did you leave and when did you return?**
    - I left on (month / day / year) and returned on (month / day / year).

- **Where did you go?**
    - I went to (name of country).

- **Why did you go?**
    - I went to visit my family.
    - I went on vacation.
    - I went on business.

- **What ocean is on the West Coast of the United States?**
    - Pacific Ocean

Practice D: Nobility

- **Do you have any title of nobility in a foreign country?**
    - No, I don't.

- **What is "nobility"?**
    - Nobility is to be a member of the family of a king or queen.

- **What did the Declaration of Independence do?**
    - Announced our independence from Great Britain.

Practice E: Legally Incompetent

- **Have you been declared legally incompetent?**

  - No, never.

- **What is "legally incompetent"?**

  - I am too sick to make my own decisions. A judge says that a legal guardian, such as family member, doctor, or lawyer, must make decisions for me.

- **What does the judicial branch of the government do?**

  - Decides if a law goes against the Constitution.

Practice F: Groups, Communism, Terrorism

- **Do you belong to any groups or organizations?**
  - Yes, I belong to (name of group).
  - Yes, I am a member of a (church, mosque, temple).
  - Yes, I am a member of a labor union.
  - Yes, I belong to a parent-teacher group at my children's school.
  - Yes, I play on a sports team.
  - Yes, I volunteer at (name of place).

- **Have you ever been a communist?**

  - No, never.

- **What is communism?**

  - Communism is a government with a state-planned economy such as China, Vietnam, North Korea, and Cuba.

- **Have you ever been a terrorist?**

  - No, never.

- **During the Cold War, what was the main concern of the United States?**

  - Communism

Practice G: Habitual Drunkard and Illegal Drugs

- **Have you ever been a habitual drunkard?**

  - No, never.

- **What is a "habitual drunkard"?**

  - A habitual drunkard drinks too much alcohol every day and gets sick. A habitual drunkard is addicted to alcohol.

- **Have you ever used, sold, or smuggled illegal drugs?**

  - No, never.

- **What are "illegal drugs"?**

  - Illegal drugs are drugs that are against the law, such as heroin or cocaine.

- **What are two ways that Americans can participate in their democracy?**

  - Join a civic group or join a community group.

Practice H: Illegal Gambling

- **Have you ever gambled illegally?**

  - No, never.

- **What is illegal gambling?**

  - Illegal gambling is to play games such as poker or dice to win a lot of money, but not pay any taxes.

- **What is one promise you make when you become a United States citizen?**

  - Obey the laws of the United States.

Thirty-Five N-400 Questions and Eight Civics Questions

1. **Explain how you are eligible to become a US Citizen.**

   – I am over 18 years old and I have been a Legal Permanent Resident for 5 years.

   – I am over 18 years old and I have been a Legal Permanent Resident for 3 years and married to a US citizen for 3 years.

2. **What is your current legal name?**

   – My current legal name is (first name / middle name / last name).

3. **What is your date of birth?**

   – My date of birth is (month / day / year).

4. **What is your date of permanent residence?**

   – My date of permanent residence is (month / day / year)

5. **What is your country of birth?**

   – My country of birth is (name of country).

6. **What is your country of nationality?**

   – My country of nationality is (name of country).

7. **What was your port of entry?**

   – My port of entry was (airport or border crossing where you entered the US).

8. **What is your current home address?**

   – My current home address is (house number / street name / apartment number / city / state / zip code).

9. **What was your previous home address?**

   – My home previous address was (house number / street name / apartment number / city / state / zip code).
   – I don't have a previous home address.

10. **What do you do for a living?**

    – I work.
    – I go to school.
    – My spouse works.
    – My family supports me.
    – I am retired. I get a pension.
    – I am retired. I get a Social Security check.
    – I am disabled. I get a Social Security check.
    – I am unemployed. I get Unemployment.

11. **Have you taken on any trips outside of the US?**

    – Yes, I took one trip outside of the US.
    – Yes, I took (number) trips outside of the US. (Go to the next section.)
    – No, I have not taken any trips outside of the US.

12. **How many total days were you outside of the US?**

    – I was outside the US for (number) days.

13. **Tell me about your last trip: when did you leave and when did you return?**

    – I left on (month / day / year) and returned on (month / day / year).

14. **Where did you go?**

    – I went to (name of country).

15. **Why did you go?**

    – I went to visit my family.
    – I went on vacation.
    – I went on business

16. **What is your marital status?**

- I am single.
- I am married.
- I am widowed.
- I am divorced.

17. **Do you have children?**

- I have one child.
- I have (number) children.
- I don't have any children.

18. **Have you ever claimed to be a US citizen?**

- No, I have never claimed to be a US citizen.

19. **Do you have any title of nobility in a foreign country?**

- No, I don't.

20. **What is "nobility"?**

- Nobility is to be a member of the family of a king or queen.

21. **Have you been declared legally incompetent?**

- No, I have never been declared legally incompetent.

22. **What is "legally incompetent"?**

- I am too sick to make my own decisions. A judge says that a legal guardian, such as family member, doctor, or lawyer, must make decisions for me.

23. **Do you belong to any groups or organizations?**

- Yes, I belong to (name of group).
- Yes, I am a member of a (church, mosque, temple).
- Yes, I am a member of a labor union.
- Yes, I belong to a parent-teacher group at my children's school.
- Yes, I play on a sports team.
- Yes, I volunteer at (name of place).

24. **Have you ever been a communist?**

   – No, I have never been a communist.

25. **What is communism?**

   – The Government Party with a state-planned economy, such as China, Vietnam, North Korea, and Cuba.

26. **Have you ever been a terrorist?**

   – No, I have never been a terrorist.

27. **Have you ever been a habitual drunkard?**

   – No, I have never been a habitual drunkard.

28. **What is a "habitual drunkard"?**

   – A habitual drunkard drinks too much alcohol every day and gets sick. A habitual drunkard is addicted to alcohol.

29. **Have you ever used, sold, or smuggled illegal drugs?**

   – No, I have never used, sold, or smuggled illegal drugs.

30. **What are "illegal drugs"?**

   – Illegal drugs are drugs that are against the law, such as heroin or cocaine.

31. **Have you ever gambled illegally?**

   – No, I have never gambled illegally.

32. **What is "illegal gambling"?**

   – Illegal gambling is to play games such as poker or dice to win a lot of money, but not pay any taxes.

33. **Do you support the Constitution and the US government?**

   – Yes, I support the Constitution.

34. **If the law requires it, are you willing to bear arms in the US armed forces?**

   – Yes, I am willing to bear arms.

35. **If the law requires it, are you willing to perform noncombatant services for the US armed forces?**

– Yes, I am willing to perform noncombatant services.

Civics Questions

1. **Name one state that borders Canada.**

– Answer:_____

2. **What are two Cabinet-level positions?**

– Answer:_____

3. **What ocean is on the West Coast of the United States?**

– Answer:_____

4. **What did the Declaration of Independence do?**

– Answer:_____

5. **What does the judicial branch of the government do?**

– Answer:_____

6. **During the Cold War, what was the main concern of the United States?**

– Answer:_____

7. **What are two ways that Americans can participate in their democracy?**

– Answer:_____

8. **What is one promise you make when you become a United States citizen?**

– Answer:_____

Interview 8: Forty N-400 Questions and Eight Civics Questions

Vocabulary:

Ex-Spouse	Freedom of Speech	School
Financial Support	House of Representatives	Spouse
Freedom of Religion	Retired	Work of Nat'l Importance

Write the correct vocabulary under each picture.

1.

2.

3.

4.

5.

6.

7.

8.

9.

Vocabulary:

Ex-Spouse	Freedom of Speech	School
Financial Support	House of Representatives	Spouse
Freedom of Religion	Retired	Work of Nat'l Importance

Write the vocabulary next to the definition.

1. _____: How I pay for my living expenses, such as food and rent.
Example: I have a full-time job. I pay the expenses for my wife, our children, plus I send money to my parents in Mexico.

2. _____: My current husband or wife.
Example: I am married. I have a husband and I am my husband's wife.

3. _____: My previous husband or wife.
Example: I have been married two times. I divorced my first husband and married my current husband.

4. _____: The lower house of the US Congress.
Example: There are 435 voting members in the US Congress. Some states have more representatives because they have more people.

5. _____: The right to say what we think.
Example: In a democracy, people are free to think and say what they want.

6. _____: To do work to support our nation under civilian direction.
Example: I am a computer programmer. My company helps the government stop cyber-attacks. On weekends, my co-workers and I volunteer for the Red Cross.

7. _____: To go to a college, university, or training program full-time.
Example: I am studying to become a registered nurse. I will graduate next year.

8. _____: To leave a job and not work anymore.
Example: After running my company for over 25 years, I stopped working and turned over the business to my children.

9. _____: We can practice any religion or not practice a religion.
Example: I am Catholic and my husband is Buddhist. We go to church every Sunday and to temple on Vietnamese holidays.

Practice Questions

Practice A: Financial Support

- **How do you financially support yourself?**
  - I work at (company name).
  - I go to school at (school name).
  - My spouse works at (company name).
  - My family supports me.
  - I am retired. I get a pension.
  - I am retired. I get a Social Security check.
  - I am disabled. I get a Social Security check.
  - I am unemployed. I get an Unemployment check.

- **What is freedom of religion?**
  - You can practice any religion, or not practice a religion.

Practice B: Marital Status, Spouse, and Ex-Spouse

- **What is your marital status?**
  - I am single. (Go to the next section.)
  - I am married.
  - I am widowed.
  - I am divorced.

- **How many times have times have you been married?**
  - I have been married one time.
  - I have been married (number) of times.

- **What is the name of your current spouse?**
  - My (husband's / wife's) name is (first name / middle name / last name).

- **Is (he / she) a US citizen?**
  - Yes, (he / she) became a US on (month / day / year) at (city / state).
  - No, (he /she) is not a US citizen.

- **If you have been married before, what is the name of your previous spouse? (Repeat for each ex-spouse.)**
  - My (ex-husband's / ex-wife's) name is (first name / middle name / last name).

- **Has your current spouse been married before?**
  - Yes
  - No

- **If your spouse has been married before, what is the name of (his / her) previous spouse? (Repeat for each ex-spouse.)**
  - Her ex-husband's name is (first name / middle name / last name).
  - His ex-wife's name is (first name / middle name / last name).

- **What are two rights of everyone living in the United States?**
  - Freedom of speech and freedom of religion.

Practice C: Children

- **Do you have any children?**
  - I have one child.
  - I have (number) children.
  - I don't have any children. (Go to the next section.)

- **What is your child's name?**
  - My (first / second / third...) child's name is (first name / middle name / last name). (Repeat for each child.)

- **Was your child born in the US?**
  - My (first / second / third . . .) child was born in (name of country). (Repeat for each child.)

- **Is your child a US citizen?**

  - My (first / second / third . . .) child is a US citizen because (he / she) was born in the US. (Repeat for each child.)
  - My (first / second / third . . .) child is a US citizen because (his / her) father is a US citizen. (Repeat for each child.)
  - My (first / second / third . . .) child is a US citizen because (his / her) mother is a US citizen. (Repeat for each child.)
  - My (first / second / third . . .) child is not a US citizen. (Repeat for each child.)

- **The House of Representatives has how many voting members?**

  - Four hundred thirty-five (435).

Practice D: The Constitution and the US Form of Government

- **Do you support the Constitution and the US form of government?**

  - Yes

- **What is the Constitution?**

  - The Constitution is the supreme law of the land.

- **What is the US form of government?**

  - The US has a democratic form of government.

- **What stops one branch of government from becoming too powerful?**

  - Checks and balances.

Practice E: Oath of Allegiance

- **Do you understand the full Oath of Allegiance to the United States?**

  - Yes

- **What is an "oath"?**

  - An oath is a solemn promise.

- **What is "allegiance"?**
  - Allegiance is loyalty.

- **What is the full Oath of Allegiance?**
  - I promise to be loyal to the United States.

- **Are you willing to take the full Oath of Allegiance?**
  - Yes, I am willing to take the full Oath of Allegiance.
  - No, my religion prohibits the taking of oaths.

- **What do we show loyalty to when we say the Pledge of Allegiance?**
  - The United States

Practice F: Bear Arms

- **If the law requires it, are you willing to bear arms in the US armed forces?**
  - Yes, I am.
  - No, my religion prohibits the use of weapons.

- **What is "bear arms"?**
  - Bear arms is to use a weapon to protect the country.

- **Give an example of bearing arms.**
  - For example, to fight in the US armed services as soldier or Marine.

- **Who is the Commander in Chief of the military?**
  - The President

Practice G: Noncombatant

- **If the law requires it, are you willing to perform noncombatant services for the US armed forces?**
  - Yes, I am.
  - No, my religion prohibits service in the armed forces.

- **What is "noncombatant"?**

  – Noncombatant is to work in the US armed forces without using weapons.

- **Give an example of noncombatant service.**

  – For example, to work in the US armed services as a cook, translator, or computer programmer.

- **If the President can no longer serve, who becomes President?**

  – The Vice President

Practice H: Work of National Importance

- **If the law requires it, are you willing to do work of national importance under civilian direction?**

  – Yes, I am.

- **Give an example of work of national importance under civilian direction.**

  – For example, help the Red Cross in an emergency, such as a flood or earthquake; or do computer programming for national security projects.

- **What is one promise you make when you become a United States citizen?**

  – Serve (do important work for) the nation (if needed).

Forty N-400 Questions and Eight Civics Questions

N-400 Questions

1. **Explain how you are eligible to become a US Citizen.**

   – I am over 18 years old and I have been a Legal Permanent Resident for 5 years.
   – I am over 18 years old and I have been a Legal Permanent Resident for 3 years, and married to a US citizen for 3 years.

2. **What is your date of birth?**

   – My date of birth is (month / day / year).

3. **What is your date of permanent residence?**

   – My date of permanent residence is (month / day / year).

4. **What is your country of birth?**

   – My country of birth is (name of country).

5. **What is your country of nationality?**

   – My country of nationality is (name of country).

6. **What is your home address now?**

   – My home address is (house number / street name / apartment number / city / state / zip code).

7. **What was your home address before?**

   – My home address before was (house number / street name / apartment number / city / state / zip code).
   – I have only lived at (house number / street name / apartment number / city / state / zip code).

8. **How do you financially support yourself?**

   – I work at (company name).
   – I go to school at (school name).

- My spouse works at (company name).
- My family supports me.
- I am retired. I get a pension.
- I am retired. I get a Social Security check.
- I am disabled. I get a Social Security check.
- I am unemployed. I get an Unemployment check.

9. What is your marital status?

- I am single. (Go to the next section.)
- I am married.
- I am widowed.
- I am divorced.

10. How many times have times have you been married?

- I have been married one time.
- I have been married (number) of times.

11. What is the name of your current spouse?

- My (husband's / wife's) name is (first name / middle name / last name).

12. Is (he / she) a US citizen?

- Yes, (he / she) became a US on (month / day / year) at (city / state).
- No, (he /she) is not a US citizen.

13. If you have been married before, what is the name of your previous spouse? (Repeat for each ex-spouse.)

- My (ex-husband's / ex-wife's) name is (first name / middle name / last name).

14. Has your current spouse been married before?

- Yes
- No

15. If your spouse has been married before, what is the name of (his / her) previous spouse? (Repeat for each ex-spouse.)

- Her ex-husband's name is (first name / middle name / last name).

– His ex-wife's name is (first name / middle name / last name).

16. **Do you have any children?**

– I have one child.
– I have (number) children.
– I don't have any children. (Go to the next section.)

17. **What is your child's name?**

– My (first / second / third . . .) child's name is (first name / middle name / last name). (Repeat for each child.)

18. **Was your child born in the US?**

– My (first / second / third . . .) child was born in (name of country). (Repeat for each child.)

19. **Is your child a US citizen?**

– My (first / second / third . . .) child is a US citizen because (he / she) was born in the US (Repeat for each child.)
– My (first / second / third . . .) child is a US citizen because (his / her) father is a US citizen. (Repeat for each child.)
– My (first / second / third . . .) child is a US citizen because (his / her) mother is a US citizen. (Repeat for each child.)
– My (first / second / third . . .) child is not a US citizen. (Repeat for each child.)

20. **Have you ever claimed to be a US citizen?**

– No, I have never claimed to be a US citizen.

21. **Do you pay your income taxes every year?**

– Yes, I pay my income taxes ever year.
– No, I don't pay taxes because I have no income.

22. **Have you ever been a terrorist or committed any acts of violence?**

– No, I have never been a terrorist or committed any acts of violence.

23. Have you ever been arrested or committed any crimes?

    – No, I have never been arrested or committed any crimes.

    – Yes, I was arrested (month / day / year) at (city / state) for (name of the crime). Here are my court records.

24. Do you support the Constitution and the US form of government?

    – Yes, I support the Constitution and the US form or government.

25. What is the Constitution?

    – The Constitution is the supreme law of the land.

26. What is the US form of government?

    – The US has a democratic form of government.

27. Do you understand the full Oath of Allegiance to the United States?

    – Yes, I am willing to take the full Oath of Allegiance.

28. What is an "oath"?

    – An oath is a solemn promise.

29. What is "allegiance"?

    – Allegiance is loyalty.

30. What is the full Oath of Allegiance?

    – I promise to be loyal to the United States.

31. Are you willing to take the full Oath of Allegiance?

    – Yes, I am willing to take the full Oath of Allegiance.

    – No, my religion prohibits the taking of oaths.

32. If the law requires it, are you willing to bear arms in the US armed forces?

    – Yes, I am willing to bear arms in the US armed forces.

    – No, my religion prohibits the use of weapons.

33. **What is "bear arms"?**

   – Bear arms is to use a weapon to protect the country.

34. **Give an example of bearing arms.**

   – For example, to fight in the US armed services as soldier or Marine.

35. **If the law requires it, are you willing to perform noncombatant services for the US armed forces?**

   – Yes, I am willing to perform noncombatant services for the US armed forces.
   – No, my religion prohibits service in the armed forces.

36. **What is "noncombatant"?**

   – Noncombatant is to work in the US armed forces without using weapons.

37. **Give an example of noncombatant service.**

   – For example work in the US armed services as a cook, translator, or computer programmer.

38. **If the law requires it, are you willing to do work of national importance under civilian direction?**

   – Yes, I am willing to do work of national importance.

39. **Give an example of work of national importance under civilian direction.**

   – For example, help the Red Cross in an emergency like a flood or earthquake, or do computer programming for national security projects.

40. **Do you promise that everything that you said is true?**

   – Yes, I promise that everything that I said is true.

Civics Questions

1. **What is freedom of religion?**

   – Answer:_____

2. **What are two rights of everyone living in the United States?**

    – Answer:_____

3. **The House of Representatives has how many voting members?**

    – Answer:_____

4. **What stops one branch of government from becoming too powerful?**

    – Answer:_____

5. **What do we show loyalty to when we say the Pledge of Allegiance?**

    – Answer:_____

6. **Who is the Commander in Chief of the military?**

    – Answer:_____

7. **If the President can no longer serve, who becomes President?**

    – Answer:_____

8. **What is one promise you make when you become a United States citizen?**

    – Answer:_____

Interview 9: Forty-Five N-400 Questions and Nine Civics Questions

Vocabulary:

Child Soldier	Military	Slavery
Gang	Rebel	US Armed Forces
Life and Liberty	Selective Service	Weapons

Write the correct vocabulary under each picture.

1.

2.

3.

4.

5.

6.

7.

8.

9.

Vocabulary:

Child Soldier   Military   Slavery
Gang   Rebel   US Armed Forces
Life and Liberty   Selective Service   Weapons

Write the vocabulary next to the definition.

1. _____: A child under 15 years old who fights in the armed forces.
   Example: The opposition kidnapped young boys and forced them to fight.

2. _____: A group that uses weapons to fight against the government.
   Example: During a civil war, the opposition fights against the official government's armed forces for control of the country.

3. _____: A group that uses violence against people.
   Example: The criminals recruited teenagers to sell drugs. If teens refused, they were beaten up by the criminals.

4. _____: All young men between their 18th and 26th birthdays must register with "the Draft" (SSS.gov). These young men will be called to join the armed forces if there is a national emergency.
   Example: I am a male who came to the US when I was 19. I registered for "the Draft" on my birthday. Here is my SSS number.

5. _____: An object that can hurt or kill people or property.
   Example: When I was in the US Marines, I was trained to use guns. When I was on duty, I carried a rifle to protect the soldiers in my unit.

6. _____: To live and be free.
   Example: All people want to live and be free.

7. _____: The official armed forces of the national government.
   Example: Before I came to the US, I served two years in the South Korean Navy.

8. _____: To be a member of the United States Army, Navy, Air Force, Marines, or Coast Guard.
   Example: My son joined the US Army, served in Iraq, became a US citizen, and then petitioned for our family to become US citizens.

9. _____: To buy, sell, and own people. To take away a person's rights and force them to work without pay.
   Example: From 1619-1808, Africans were brought to America. Instead of freeing the Africans and their children, their masters continued to force them to work. This was one of the problems that led to the Civil War (1861-1865).

Practice Questions

Practice A: Hurt or Kill on Purpose

- **Have you ever badly hurt or killed a person on purpose?**

  – No, never.

- **What is to "hurt or kill on purpose"?**

  – A person *plans* to hurt or kill a person *and then does it.*

- **What are two rights in the Declaration of Independence?**

  – Life and liberty.

Practice B: Military Service

- **Have you ever participated in a military unit, paramilitary, or rebel group?**

  – Yes, I served in the armed forces in my country.
  – No, I never served in the armed forces in my country.

- **What is a "military unit"?**

  – A military unit is the official armed forces of the national government that protects the country.

- **What is a "paramilitary unit"?**

  – A paramilitary unit is a group of people who act like the military, but are not a part of the official armed forces of the national government.

- **What is a "rebel group"?**

  – A rebel group fights against the official government.

- **Under our Constitution, some powers belong to the federal government. What is one power of the federal government?**

  – To create an army.

Practice C: Work in a Prison

- **Have you ever worked in a place like a prison or labor camp?**
  - No, never.

- **What is a "prison camp"?**
  - Prisoners must work, or they are killed or tortured.

- **Who makes federal laws?**
  - Congress

Practice D: Gang

- **Have you ever been a member of a gang?**
  - No, never.

- **What is a "gang"?**
  - A gang is a group of criminals.

- **How many justices are on the Supreme Court?**
  - Nine (9)

Practice E: Weapons

- **Have you ever sold or given weapons to another person?**
  - No, never.

- **What are "weapons"?**
  - Weapons are guns, bombs, or anything that can hurt or kill another person.

- **What are two rights of everyone living in the United States?**
  - Freedom to petition the government and the right to bear arms.

Practice F: Military or Weapons Training

- **Have you ever received military or weapons training?**
    - Yes, I have received weapons training.
    - Yes, I learned a how to use a gun for personal protection and I have a gun permit.
    - No, never.

- **What is "military training"?**
    - A person learns how to use a weapon in the national armed forces to protect the country.

- **Name one war fought by the United States in the 1900s.**
    - Vietnam War

Practice G: Child Soldiers

- **Have you ever forced a child (under 15) to become a soldier or to help soldiers?**
    - No, never.

- **What is a "child soldier"?**
    - A child soldier is a child under 15 years old who fights in a militia, army, or rebel group.

- **How can a child help soldiers?**
    - A child is a cook, porter, servant, etc. for soldiers.

- **Name one problem that led to the Civil War.**
    - Slavery

Practice H: Selective Service

- **Are you a male who lived in the US between your 18th and 26th birthdays?**

  – Yes, I am a male who lived in the US between my 18th and 26th birthdays.

  – I am male, but I came to the US after my 26th birthday.

  – I am female.

- **If yes, when did you registered to the Selective Service?**

  – I registered on (month / day / year). This is my SSS.gov number.

  – I did not register because I didn't know about the Selective Service.

  – I did not register because military service is against my religion. Here is a letter from my religious elder.

- **When must all men register for the Selective Service?**

  – Between eighteen (18) and twenty-six (26).

Practice I: US Armed Forces

- **Have you ever served in the US armed forces?**

  – Yes, I served in the US armed forces.

  – I worked for the US armed forces.

  – I never served in the US armed forces.

- **Give an example of the US armed forces.**

  – To bear arms as a combatant or serve as a noncombatant in the United States Army, Navy, Air Force, Marines, or Coast Guard.

- **What is one promise you make when you become a United States citizen?**

  – Serve in the US military (if needed).

Forty-Five N-400 Questions and Nine Civics Questions

N-400 Questions

1. **Explain how you are eligible to become a US Citizen.**

   – I am over 18 years old and I have been a Legal Permanent Resident for 5 years.
   – I am over 18 years old and I have been a Legal Permanent Resident for 3 years, and married to a US citizen for 3 years.
   – I am applying for US Citizenship based on Qualifying Military Service.

2. **What is your full name?**

   – My full name is (first name / middle name / last name).

3. **What is your date of birth?**

   – My date of birth is (month / day / year).

4. **What is your date of permanent residence?**

   – My date of permanent residence is (month / day / year).

5. **What is your country of birth?**

   – My country of birth is (name of country).

6. **What is your country of nationality?**

   – My country of nationality is (name of country).

7. **What is your current home address?**

   – My home address is (house number / street name / apartment number / city / state / zip code).

8. **How do you financially support yourself?**

   – I work at (company name).
   – I go to school at (school name).
   – My spouse works at (company name).

- My family supports me.
- I am retired. I get a pension.
- I am retired. I get a Social Security check.
- I am disabled. I get a Social Security check.
- I am unemployed. I get an Unemployment check.

9.   Have you traveled outside of the United States?

- Yes, I left (month / date / year) and returned.
- No, I haven't traveled outside of the United States. (Go to the next section.)

10.   What is your marital status?

- I am single. (Go to the next section.)
- I am married.
- I am widowed.
- I am divorced.

11.   Do you have any children?

- I have one child.
- I have (number) children.
- I don't have any children. (Go to the next section.)

12.   Have you ever claimed to be a US citizen?

- No, I have never claimed to be a US citizen.

13.   Do you pay your income taxes every year?

- Yes, I pay my income taxes ever year.
- No, I don't pay taxes because I have no income.

14.   Have you ever been a terrorist or committed any acts of violence?

- No, I have never been a terrorist or committed any acts of violence.

15.   Have you ever badly hurt or killed a person on purpose?

- No, I have never badly hurt or killed a person on purpose.

16.   What is to "hurt or kill on purpose"?

–   A person plans to hurt or kill a person and then does it.

17.   Have you ever participated in a military unit, paramilitary, or rebel group?

–   Yes, I served in the armed forces in my country.
–   No, I never served in the armed forces in my country.

18.   What is a "military unit"?

–   A military unit is the official armed forces of the national government that protects the country.

19.   What is a "paramilitary unit"?

–   A paramilitary unit is a group of people who act like the military, but are not a part of the official armed forces of the national government.

20.   What is a rebel group?

–   A rebel group fights against the official government.

21.   Have you ever worked in a place like a prison or labor camp?

–   No, I have never worked in a place like a prison or labor camp.

22.   What is a "prison camp"?

–   Prisoners must work or they are killed or tortured.

23.   Have you ever been a member of a gang?

–   No, I have never been a member of a gang.

24.   What is a "gang"?

–   A gang is a group of criminals.

25.   Have you ever sold or given weapons to another person?

–   No, I have never sold or given weapons to another person.

26.   What are "weapons"?

–   Weapons are guns, bombs, or anything that can hurt or kill another person.

27. **Have you ever received military or weapons training?**

- Yes, I have received weapons training.
- Yes, I learned a how to use a gun for personal protection and I have a gun permit.
- No, I have never received military or weapons training.

28. **What is "military training"?**

- A person learns how to use a weapon in the national armed forces to protect the country.

29. **Have you ever forced a child (under 15) to become a soldier or to help soldiers?**

- No, I have never forced a child to become a soldier or to help soldiers.

30. **What is a "child soldier"?**

- A child soldier is a child under 15 years old who fights in a militia, army, or rebel group.

31. **How can a child help soldiers?**

- A child is a cook, porter, servant, etc. for soldiers.

32. **Have you ever been arrested or committed any crimes?**

- No, I have never been arrested or committed any crimes.
- Yes, I was arrested (month / day / year) at (city / state) for (name of the crime). Here are my court records.

33. **Have you ever been deported?**

- No, have never been deported.

34. **Are you a male who lived in the US between your 18th and 26th birthdays?**

- Yes, I am a male who lived in the US between my 18th and 26th birthdays.
- I am male, but I came to the US after my 26th birthday.
- I am female.

35. **If yes, when did you registered to the Selective Service?**

- I registered on (month / day / year). This is my SSS.gov number.
- I did not register because I didn't know about the Selective Service.
- I did not register because military service is against my religion. Here is a letter from my religious elder.

36. **Have you ever served in the US armed forces?**

- Yes, I served in the US armed forces.
- I worked for the US armed forces.
- I never served in the US armed forces.

37. **Give an example of the US armed forces.**

- To bear arms as a combatant or serve as a noncombatant in the United States Army, Navy, Air Force, Marines, or Coast Guard.

38. **Do you support the Constitution and the US form of government?**

- Yes, I support the Constitution and the US form or government.

39. **Are you willing to take the full Oath of Allegiance?**

- Yes, I am willing to take the full Oath of Allegiance.
- No, my religion prohibits the taking of oaths.

40. **If the law requires it, are you willing to bear arms in the US armed forces?**

- Yes, I am willing to bear arms in the US armed forces.
- No, my religion prohibits the use of weapons.

41. **What is "bear arms"?**

- Bear arms is to use a weapon to protect the country.

42. **If the law requires it, are you willing to perform noncombatant services for the US armed forces?**

- Yes, I am willing to perform noncombatant services for the US armed forces.
- No, my religion prohibits service in the armed forces.

43. What is "noncombatant"?

— Noncombatant is to work in the US armed forces without using weapons.

44. If the law requires it, are you willing to do work of national importance under civilian direction?

— Yes, I will do work of national importance under civilian direction.

45. Do you promise that everything that you said is true?

— Yes, everything is true.

Civics Questions

1. What are two rights in the Declaration of Independence?

— Answer:_____

2. Under our Constitution, some powers belong to the federal government. What is one power of the federal government?

— Answer:_____

3. Who makes federal laws?

— Answer:_____

4. How many justices are on the Supreme Court?

— Answer:_____

5. What are two rights of everyone living in the United States?

— Answer:_____

6. Name one war fought by the United States in the 1900s.

— Answer:_____

7. Name one problem that led to the Civil War.

— Answer:_____

8. **When must all men register for the Selective Service?**

   – Answer:_____

9. **What is one promise you make when you become a United States citizen?**

   – Answer:_____

Interview 10: Fifty N-400 Questions and Ten Civics Questions

Vocabulary:

Become a US Citizen
Civil Rights
Freedom of the Press

Illegal Entry
Miss
Oath of Allegiance

Persecute
Small Talk
Women's Rights

Write the correct vocabulary under each picture.

1.

2.

3.

4.

5.

6.

7.

8.

9.

Vocabulary:

Become a US Citizen	Illegal Entry	Persecute
Civil Rights	Miss	Small Talk
Freedom of the Press	Oath of Allegiance	Women's Rights

Write the vocabulary next to the definition.

1. _____: Polite, friendly conversation about unimportant topics.
   Example: Before the interview, the USCIS officer asked me a few simple questions about traffic, the weather, and my family. I think she knew that I was nervous, and that talking about these topics helped me calm down.

2. _____: To feel sad because someone is not with you.
   Example: What do I miss about my home country? I am sad that my parents are in Vietnam and want them to come here to live with me.

3. _____: A solemn promise to be loyal to the United States.
   Example: I promise to be loyal to the United States.

4. _____: Equal access to schools, jobs, and government services.
   Example: Susan B. Anthony worked for women to have the right to vote.

5. _____: People are free to write and publish what they want.
   Example: People write to their newspaper to express their opinions about politics.

6. _____: The rights that every person should have, such as the right to vote or to be treated fairly by the law.
   Example: Martin Luther King Jr. worked for equality for all Americans.

7. _____: To hate and hurt someone because he or she belongs to different race, religion, group, gender, sexual orientation, or political party, etc.
   Example: I don't hate anyone because they are different.

8. _____: To help others come into the United States without a proper visa or to stay in the US on an expired visa.
   Example: The Border Patrol arrested a ship's crew that was trying to smuggle people into the US.

9. _____: The reason you want to change your Citizenship.
   Example: Why do I want to become an American? I came to America to live in freedom. And I want a better life for my children.

Practice Questions

Practice A: Introduction and "Small Talk"

- **Hi. I am Officer (last name). I will be interviewing you today.**
  - Hi, my name is (first name / last name).

- **Why are you here today?**
  - I want to become an American citizen.

- **Why do you want to become an American citizen? (Pick one.)**
  - I love America.
  - I love freedom.
  - I want a better life for my children.
  - I want to live with my family.
  - There are good opportunities here.

- **What do you miss about your old country? (Pick one.)**
  - I miss my friends and family.
  - I miss the food.
  - I miss (person / place / thing / activity / holiday).

- **Are you ready? Do you have any questions before we begin?**
  - I am ready to begin.
  - I'm a little nervous, but I'm ready.
  - Yes, I have a question: (Ask your question).

- **Why does the flag have 50 stars?**
  - Because there is one star for each state.

Practice B: Oath to Tell the Truth

- **Do you promise to tell the truth, the whole truth, and nothing but the truth?**
  - Yes, I do.

- **What did you just promise?**

  – I promised to tell the truth.

- **What is one right or freedom from the First Amendment? (Pick one.)**

  – Speech
  – Religion
  – Assembly
  – Press
  – Petition the government

Practice C: Eligibility

- **Explain how you are eligible to become a US Citizen.**

  – I am over 18 years old and I have been a Legal Permanent Resident for 5 years.
  – I am over 18 years old and I have been a Legal Permanent Resident for 3 years and married to a US citizen for 3 years.
  – I am married to a US citizen who works for the US government and is stationed abroad (INA 319b).
  – I am applying for US Citizenship based on Qualifying Military Service.

- **Show me you Green Card, Passport, or State-issued Photo ID.**

  – Here is my Green Card and State-issued Photo ID.

- **Why do some states have more Representatives than other states?**

  – Because some states have more people.

Practice D: Name, Origin, Request for Accommodation or Exemption

- **What is your current legal name?**

  – My current legal name is (first name / middle name / last name).

- **Is the name on your Green Card the same as your current legal name?**
  - Yes, it is.
  - No. The name on my Green Card is not the same as my current legal name. The name on my Green Card is my maiden name. I got married and changed my last name.
  - No. The name on my Green Card is not the same as my current legal name because I went to court and legally changed my name.

- **What is your date of birth?**
  - My date of birth is (month / day / year).

- **When did you become a Legal Permanent Resident?**
  - I became a Legal Permanent Resident on (month / day / year).

- **What is your country of birth?**
  - My country of birth is (name of the country).

- **What is your country of nationality?**
  - My country of nationality is (name of the country on your passport).

- **Are you requesting any accommodations or exemptions?**
  - No, I am not requesting any accommodations or exemptions.
  - Yes, I am deaf/hard-of-hearing and require an ASL interpreter.
  - Yes, I use a wheelchair or mobility aid.
  - Yes, I am blind (or have low-vision).
  - Yes, I have another disability (describe the disability).

- **What is one thing Benjamin Franklin is famous for? (Pick one.)**
  - He was a US diplomat.
  - He was the oldest member of the Constitutional Convention.
  - He was the first Postmaster General of the United States.
  - He was the writer of "Poor Richard's Almanac."
  - He started the first free libraries.

Practice E: Home Address, Job, Travel

- **What is your current home address?**

  - My home address is (house number / street name / apartment number / city / state / zip code).

- **How long have you lived at your current home address?**

  - I have lived at my current home address from (month / day / year) to the present.

- **How do you make a living?**

  - I work at (name of the business).
  - I am a student at (name of the school).
  - I am disabled. I get a Social Security check.
  - I am retired. I get a Social Security check.
  - I am retired. I get a pension.
  - I am self-employed.
  - I am unemployed. I get an Unemployment check.
  - I stay at home and take care of my family.
  - I was laid off and I am looking for a job.
  - My family supports me.
  - My spouse works at (name of the business).

- **Have you taken any trips outside the US during the last 5 years?**

  - Yes, I have.
  - No, I haven't. (Skip to the next section.)

- **How many total days did you spend outside the US during the last 5 years?**

  - I haven't traveled outside the US.
  - I traveled (number) days outside of the US.

- **How many trips have you taken outside of the US during the last 5 years?**

  - I have taken (number) trips outside of the US during the past 5 years.
  - I haven't taken any trips.

- **Tell me about your last trip. When did you leave and when did you return?**
  - I left the US on (month / day / year) to (month / day / year).

- **What did Martin Luther King Jr. do?**
  - He worked for equality for all Americans.

Practice F: Marital Status and Children

- **What is your current marital status?**
  - I am single (never married).
  - I am married.
  - I am legally separated from my spouse.
  - I am divorced.
  - I am widowed.
  - My marriage was annulled.

- **What is your spouse's name?**
  - My husband's/wife's name is (first name / last name).

- **How many children do you have?**
  - I don't have any children.
  - I have one child.
  - I have (number) children.
  - I have (number) living children, (number) missing children, and (number) dead children.

- **What is your (first / second / third / . . .) child's name? (Repeat for each child.)**
  - My (first / second / third / ...) child's name is (first name / last name).

- **What did Susan B. Anthony do?**
  - She fought for women's rights.

Practice G: Intro to Part 12

- **Have you ever claimed to be a US citizen?**
    - No, never.

- **Have you ever voted in any US elections?**
    - No, never.

- **Have you been declared legally incompetent?**
    - No, never.

- **Have you ever failed to file your taxes?**
    - No, never.

- **Do you owe any taxes?**
    - No, I don't.

- **There are four amendments to the Constitution about who can vote. Describe one of them.**
    - You don't have to pay (a poll tax) to vote.

Practice H: Membership

- **Do you belong to any groups or organizations?**
    - Yes, I do. I belong to (name of the organization).
    - I belong to a labor union.
    - No, I don't.

- **Have you ever been a member of the Communist party?**
    - No, never.
    - Yes, I used to belong to the Communist party for my job.
    - Yes, I used to belong to the Communist party because it was compulsory.

- **Have you ever been a terrorist?**
    - No, never.

- **Have you ever badly hurt or killed a person on purpose?**
  - – No, never.

- **Have you ever persecuted any person because of race, religion, social group, or political party?**
  - – No, never.

- **What is "persecute"?**
  - – Persecute is to hate and hurt someone because he or she belongs to a different race, religion, group, or political party.

- **What movement tried to end racial discrimination?**
  - – The Civil Rights movement

Practice I: Crime

- **Have you ever been arrested or committed a crime?**
  - – No, never.

- **Have you ever been a habitual drunkard?**
  - – No, never.

- **Have you ever sold or smuggled illegal drugs or narcotics?**
  - – No, never.

- **Have you ever helped anyone enter the US illegally?**
  - – No, never.

- **Have you ever been deported?**
  - – No, never.

- **Who did the United States fight in World War II?**
  - – Japan, Germany, and Italy

Practice J: Attachment to the Constitution

- **Do you support the Constitution and the form of government of the US?**
  - Yes, I do.

- **Are you willing to take the full Oath of Allegiance to the US government?**
  - Yes, I am.

- **If the law requires it, are you willing to bear arms in the US armed forces?**
  - Yes, I am.

- **What is "to bear arms"?**
  - I will use a weapon to protect the US if required by law.

- **Are you willing to perform noncombatant services for the US armed forces?**
  - Yes, I am.

- **What is "noncombatant"?**
  - I will help the US armed forces without using a weapon.

- **Are you willing to help the government during a national emergency?**
  - Yes, I am.

- **Do you promise that everything you said is true?**
  - Yes, I do.

- **What is one promise you make when you become a United States citizen?**
  - I promise to be loyal to the United States.

Fifty N-400 Questions and Ten Civics Questions

- **Hi. I am Officer (last name). I will be interviewing you today.**
  - Hi, my name is (first name / last name).

1. **Why are you here today?**
   - I want to become an American citizen.

2. **Why do you want to become an American citizen? (Pick one.)**
   - I love America.
   - I love freedom.
   - I want a better life for my children.
   - I want to live with my family.
   - There are good opportunities here.

3. **What do you miss about your old country? (Pick one.)**
   - I miss my friends and family.
   - I miss the food.
   - I miss (person / place / thing / activity / holiday).

4. **Are you ready? Do you have any questions before we begin?**
   - I am ready to begin.
   - I'm a little nervous, but I'm ready.
   - Yes, I have a question: (Ask your question.)

5. **Do you promise to tell the truth, the whole truth, and nothing but the truth?**
   - Yes, I do.

6. **What did you just promise?**
   - I promised to tell the truth.

7. **Explain how you are eligible to become a US citizen.**

   – I am over 18 years old and I have been a Legal Permanent Resident for 5 years.

   – I am over 18 years old and I have been a Legal Permanent Resident for 3 years, and married to a US citizen for 3 years.

   – I am married to a US citizen who works for the US government and is stationed abroad (INA 319b).

   – I am applying for US Citizenship based on Qualifying Military Service.

8. **Show me you Green Card, Passport, or State-issued Photo ID.**

   – Here is my Green Card and State-issued Photo ID.

9. **What is your current legal name?**

   – My current legal name is (first name / middle name / last name).

10. **Is the name on your Green Card the same as your current legal name?**

    – Yes, my legal name is the same as the name on my Green Card.

    – No. The name on my Green Card is not the same as my current legal name. The name on my Green Card is my maiden name. I got married and changed my last name.

    – No. The name on my Green Card is not the same as my current legal name because I went to court and legally changed my name.

11. **What is your date of birth?**

    – My date of birth is (month / day / year).

12. **When did you become a Legal Permanent Resident?**

    – I became a Legal Permanent Resident on (month / day / year).

13. **What is your country of birth?**

    – My country of birth is (name of the country).

14. **What is your country of nationality?**

    – My country of nationality is (name of the country on your passport).

15. **Are you requesting any accommodations or exemptions?**

- No, I am not requesting an accommodation or an exemption.
- Yes, I am deaf or hard-of-hearing and require an ASL interpreter.
- Yes, I use a wheelchair or a mobility aid.
- Yes, I am blind or have low-vision.
- Yes, I have another disability (describe the disability).

16. **What is your current home address?**

- My home address is (house number / street name / apartment number / city / state / zip code).

17. **How long have you lived at your current home address?**

- I have lived at my current home address from (month / day / year) to the present.

18. **How do you make a living?**

- I work at (name of the business).
- I am a student at (name of the school).
- I am disabled. I get a Social Security check.
- I am retired. I get a Social Security check.
- I am retired. I get a pension.
- I am self-employed.
- I am unemployed. I get an Unemployment check.
- I stay at home and take care of my family.
- I was laid off and I am looking for a job.
- My family supports me.
- My spouse works at (name of the business).

19. **Have you taken any trips outside the US during the last 5 years?**

- Yes, I have taken (number) trips outside the US during the last 5 years.
- No, I haven't taken any trips outside the US during the last 5 years. (Skip to the next section.)

20. **How many total days did you spend outside the US during the last 5 years?**

- I spent (number) days outside of the US during the past 5 years.
- I have not traveled outside the US.

21. **How many trips have you taken outside of the US during the last 5 years?**

- I have taken (number) trips outside of the US during the past 5 years.
- I have not taken any trips outside of the US during the past 5 years.

22. **Tell me about your last trip. When did you leave and when did you return?**

- I left the US on (month / day / year) to (month / day / year).

23. **What is your current marital status?**

- I am single (never married).
- I am married.
- I am legally separated from my spouse.
- I am divorced.
- I am widowed.
- My marriage was annulled.

24. **What is your spouse's name?**

- My husband's/wife's name is (first name / last name).

25. **How many children do you have?**

- I don't have any children.
- I have one child.
- I have (number) children.
- I have (number) living children, (number) missing children, and (number) dead children.

26. **What is your (first / second / third / . . .) child's name? (Repeat for each child.)**

- My (first / second / third / . . .) child's name is (first name / last name).

27. **Have you ever claimed to be a US citizen?**

- No, I have never claimed to be a US citizen.

28. **Have you ever voted in any US elections?**

- No, I have never voted in any US elections.

29. **Have you been declared legally incompetent?**

- No, I have never been declared legally incompetent.

30. **Have you ever failed to file your taxes?**

- No, I have never failed to file my taxes.

31. **Do you owe any taxes?**

- No, I don't owe any taxes.

32. **Do you belong to any groups or organizations?**

- Yes, I do. I belong to (name of the organization).
- I belong to a labor union.
- No, I don't belong to any groups or organizations.

33. **Have you ever been a member of the Communist party?**

- No, I have never been a member of the Communist party.
- Yes, I used to belong to the Communist party for my job.
- Yes, I used to belong to the Communist party because it was compulsory.

34. **Have you ever been a terrorist?**

- No, I have never been a terrorist.

35. **Have you ever badly hurt or killed a person on purpose?**

- No, I have never badly hurt or killed a person on purpose.

36. **Have you ever persecuted any person because of race, religion, social group, or political party?**

- No, I have never persecuted any person because of race, religion, social group, or political party.

37. What is "persecute"?

– Persecute is to hate and hurt someone because he or she belongs to different race, religion, group, or political party.

38. Have you ever been arrested or committed a crime?

– No, I have never been arrested or committed a crime.

39. Have you ever been a habitual drunkard?

– No, I have never been a habitual drunkard.

40. Have you ever sold or smuggled illegal drugs or narcotics?

– No, I have never sold or smuggled illegal drugs or narcotics.

41. Have you ever helped anyone enter the US illegally?

– No, I have never helped anyone enter the US illegally.

42. Have you ever been deported?

– No, I have never been deported.

43. Do you support the Constitution and the US form of government?

– Yes, I support the Constitution and the US form of government.

44. Are you willing to take the full Oath of Allegiance to the US government?

– Yes, I am willing to take the full Oath of Allegiance to the US government.

45. If the law requires it, are you willing to bear arms in the US armed forces?

– Yes, I am willing to bear arms in the US armed forces.

46. What is "to bear arms"?

– I will use a weapon to protect the US if required by law.

47. Are you willing to perform noncombatant services in the US armed forces?

– Yes, I am willing to perform noncombatant services in the US armed forces.

48. **What is "noncombatant"?**

– I will help the US armed forces without using a weapon.

49. **Are you willing to help the government during a national emergency?**

– Yes, I am willing to help the government during a national emergency.

50. **Do you promise that everything you said is true?**

– Yes, I promise that everything that I said is true.

Civics Questions

1. **Why does the flag have 50 stars?**

– Answer:_____

2. **What is one right or freedom from the First Amendment?**

– Answer:_____

3. **Why do some states have more Representatives than other states?**

– Answer:_____

4. **What is one thing Benjamin Franklin is famous for?**

– Answer:_____

5. **What did Martin Luther King Jr. do?**

– Answer:_____

6. **What did Susan B. Anthony do?**

– Answer:_____

7. **There are four amendments to the Constitution about who can vote. Describe one of them.**

– Answer:_____

8. **What movement tried to end racial discrimination?**

– Answer:_____

9. **Who did the United States fight in World War II?**

– Answer:_____

10. **What is one promise you make when you become a United States citizen?**

– Answer:_____

The Reading and Writing Tests

The USCIS officer will give you a paper with three sentences (interrogative sentences or questions) on it and will tell you which sentence to read aloud. You must read one sentence aloud correctly to pass the Reading Test.

IMPORTANT: There is no official list of reading sentences. Please see the Reading Vocabulary for the Naturalization Test. The list of sentences below is based on this list.

After you have read one sentence correctly, the USCIS officer will then ask you to turn over the paper and will dictate (read) one sentence for you to write. You must write one sentence correctly to pass the Writing Test. Note: Some USCIS field offices are experimenting with people writing the sentences on a tablet (iPad).

IMPORTANT: There is no official list of writing sentences. Please see the Writing Vocabulary for the Naturalization Test. The list of sentences below is based on this list.

1. Who was the second President?

    Adams was the second President.
2. What is one state next to Canada?

    Alaska is next to Canada.
3. What is the largest state?

    Alaska is the largest state.
4. Who lived here (in the US) first?

    American Indians lived here first.
5. Who is our current President?

    Donald Trump is our current President.
6. What state has the most people?

    California has the most people.
7. What is one state north of Mexico?

    California is north of Mexico.

8. What country is north of the United States?

Canada is north of the United States.

9. Who can vote?

Citizens can vote.

10. Who has the right to vote?

Citizens who are 18 and older have the right to vote.

11. When is Columbus Day?

Columbus Day is in October.

12. What does Congress do?

Congress makes laws.

13. Where does Congress meet?

Congress meets in the US Capitol Building.

14. What was one of the first 13 states?

Delaware was one of the first 13 states.

15. What was the first US state?

Delaware was the first state.

16. Name one right of everyone living in the United States.

Everyone living in the United States has freedom of speech.

17. When is Flag Day?

Flag Day is in June.

18. What is one right in the Bill of Rights?

Freedom of speech is one right in the Bill of Rights.

19. When is Independence Day?

Independence Day is in July.

20. When is Labor Day?

Labor Day is in September.

21. What President is on the five-dollar bill?

Lincoln is on the five-dollar bill.

22. Who was Abraham Lincoln?

Lincoln was the President during the Civil War.

23. When is Memorial Day?

    Memorial Day is in May.

24. What country is south of the United States?

    Mexico is south of the United States.

25. What US city has the most people?

    New York City has the most people.

26. What was the first US capital?

    New York City was the first capital.

27. Why do people come to America?

    People come here to be free.

28. What President is on the one-dollar bill?

    President Washington is on the one-dollar bill.

29. When is Presidents' Day?

    Presidents' Day is in February.

30. When is Thanksgiving?

    Thanksgiving is in November.

31. What are the colors of the flag?

    The colors of the flag are red, white, and blue.

32. Who elects Congress?

    The people elect Congress.

33. Who lives in the White House?

    The President and his family live in the White House.

34. Where does the President live?

    The President lives in the White House.

35. How many states are in the United States?

    The United States has 50 states.

36. Where is the White House?

    The White House is in Washington, D.C.

37. What is on the American flag?

    There are 13 stripes and 50 stars on the American flag.

38. How many senators are from each state?

   There are two senators from each state.

39. Why do people want to live in America?

   They want to live in a free country.

40. Why do people want to be citizens?

   They want to vote.

41. What is one state south of Canada?

   Washington State is south of Canada.

42. What state was named after George Washington?

   Washington State was named after our first President.

43. Who was the Father of Our Country?

   Washington was the Father of Our Country.

44. Who was George Washington?

   Washington was the first President of the United States.

45. Who was the first US President?

   Washington was the first US President.

46. Is Washington, D.C. a state?

   Washington, D.C. is not a state; it is the capital of the United States.

47. What is the capital of the United States?

   Washington, D.C. is the capital of the United States.

48. How many senators do we have?

   We have one hundred (100) senators.

49. What do we pay to the government?

   We pay taxes.

50. When do we vote for the President?

   We vote for the President in November.

Reading Sentences (only)

The USCIS officer will give you a paper with three sentences (interrogative sentences or questions) on it and will tell you which sentence to read aloud.

You must read one sentence aloud correctly to pass the Reading Test.

IMPORTANT: There is no official list of reading sentences. Please see the Reading Vocabulary for the Naturalization Test. The list of sentences below is based on this list.

1. Who was the second President?

2. What is one state next to Canada?

3. What is the largest state?

4. Who lived here (in the US) first?

5. Who is our current President?

6. What state has the most people?

7. What is one state north of Mexico?

8. What country is north of the United States?

9. Who can vote?

10. Who has the right to vote?

11. When is Columbus Day?

12. What does Congress do?

13. Where does Congress meet?

14. What was one of the first 13 states?

15. What was the first US state?

16. Name one right of everyone living in the United States.

17. When is Flag Day?

18. What is one right in the Bill of Rights?

19. When is Independence Day?

20. When is Labor Day?

21. What President is on the five-dollar bill?

22. Who was Abraham Lincoln?

23. When is Memorial Day?

24. What country is south of the United States?

25. What US city has the most people?

26. What was the first US capital?

27. Why do people come to America?

28. What President is on the one-dollar bill?

29. When is Presidents' Day?

30. When is Thanksgiving?

31. What are the colors of the flag?

32. Who elects Congress?

33. Who lives in the White House?

34. Where does the President live?

35. How many states are in the United States?

36. Where is the White House?

37. What is on the American flag?

38. How many senators are from each state?

39. Why do people want to live in America?

40. Why do people want to be citizens?

41. What is one state south of Canada?

42. What state was named after George Washington?

43. Who was the Father of Our Country?

44. Who was George Washington?

45. Who was the first US President?

46. Is Washington, D.C. a state?

47. What is the capital of the United States?

48. How many senators do we have?

49. What do we pay to the government?

50. When do we vote for the President?

Writing Sentences (only)

After you have read one sentence correctly, the USCIS officer will then ask you to turn over the paper and will dictate (read) one sentence for you to write. You must write one sentence correctly to pass the Writing Test. Some USCIS field offices are experimenting with people writing the sentences on a tablet (iPad).

IMPORTANT: There is no official list of writing sentences. Please see the Writing Vocabulary for the Naturalization Test. The list of sentences below is based on this list.

1. Adams was the second President.

2. Alaska is next to Canada.

3. Alaska is the largest state.

4. American Indians lived here (in the US) first.

5. Donald Trump is our current President.

6. California is the state that has the most people.

7. California is north of Mexico.

8. Canada is north of the United States.

9. Citizens can vote.

10. Citizens who are 18 and older have the right to vote.

11. Columbus Day is in October.

12. Congress makes laws.

13. Congress meets in the US Capitol Building.

14. Delaware was one of the first 13 states.

15. Delaware was the first state.

16. Everyone living in the United States has freedom of speech.

17. Flag Day is in June.

18. Freedom of speech is one right in the Bill of Rights.

19. Independence Day is in July.

20. Labor Day is in September.

21. Lincoln is on the five-dollar bill.

22. Lincoln was the President during the Civil War.

23. Memorial Day is in May.

24. Mexico is south of the United States.

25. New York City is the city that has the most people.

26. New York City was the first capital.

27. People come here to be free.

28. President Washington is on the one-dollar bill.

29. Presidents' Day is in February.

30. Thanksgiving is in November.

31. The colors of the flag are red, white, and blue.

32. The people elect Congress.

33. The President and his family live in the White House.

34. The President lives in the White House.

35. The United States has 50 states.

36. The White House is in Washington, D.C.

37. There are 13 stripes and 50 stars on the American flag.

38. There are two senators from each state.

39. They want to live in a free country.

40. They want to vote.

41. Washington State is south of Canada.

42. Washington State was named after our first President.

43. Washington was the Father of Our Country.

44. Washington was the first President of the United States.

45. Washington was the first US President.

46. Washington, D.C. is not a state; it is the capital of the United States.

47. Washington, D.C. is the capital of the United States.

48. We have 100 senators.

49. We pay taxes.

50. We vote for the President in November.

The Oath of Allegiance

The Naturalization Ceremony and the Oath of Allegiance

Congratulations! You passed your interview! But you are not a US citizen yet—you are still a Legal Permanent Resident. After your interview, the USCIS will send you a letter inviting you to a Naturalization Oath Ceremony. *You must go to your ceremony!*

At the Naturalization Oath Ceremony, you will give up your Green Card. The official ceremony begins with the singing of our national anthem, followed by some short speeches or videos about Citizenship. People start to get really excited when the host (a judge, USCIS officer, etc.) begins the "Roll Call of Nations." Stand up when you hear your country of origin. Then you will be led in the recitation of the Oath of Allegiance:

I hereby declare, on oath,

that I absolutely and entirely renounce and abjure all allegiance and fidelity to any foreign prince, potentate, state, or sovereignty, of whom or which I have heretofore been a subject or citizen;

that I will support and defend the Constitution and laws of the United States of America against all enemies, foreign and domestic;

that I will bear true faith and allegiance to the same;

that I will bear arms on behalf of the United States when required by the law;

that I will perform noncombatant service in the Armed Forces of the United States when required by the law;

that I will perform work of national importance under civilian direction when required by the law;

and that I take this obligation freely, without any mental reservation or purpose of evasion; so help me God.

Congratulations, you are now a US citizen!

After the ceremony, USCIS officers will hand you your Naturalization Certificate and you can register to vote and apply for a passport. Go out and celebrate with your family!

Getting to Know the Oath of Allegiance

The vocabulary and concepts of the Oath of Allegiance may seem difficult to understand, but there are two items that you have already studied which will help you: the USCIS 100:53 and the N-400 Part 12: 45-50. Let's review both of these items, plus learn some more vocabulary and definitions to help you be fully prepared to take the Oath of Allegiance.

USCIS 100:53

What is one promise you make when you become a United States citizen?

- be loyal to the United States
- defend the Constitution and laws of the United States
- give up loyalty to other countries
- obey the laws of the US
- serve (do important work for) the nation (if needed)
- serve in the US military (if needed)

Write the correct phrase under each picture.

1.	2.	3.
4.	5.	6.

N-400 Part 12:45-50 (formerly known as Attachment to the Constitution)

Write the correct phrase in bold under each picture.

1.	2.	3.
4.	5.	6.

45. Do you support the **US Constitution** and the **form of government**?
What is the Constitution?   It is the supreme law of the land.
What is the US form of gov't?   The US is a democracy.

46. Do you understand the full **Oath of Allegiance** to the United States?
What is an oath?   An oath is a promise.
What is allegiance?   Allegiance is to be loyal.
What is the Oath of Allegiance? I promise to be loyal to the US.

47. Are you willing to take the full Oath of Allegiance?
Will you fulfill your responsibilities   I am taking the oath freely and will fulfill
of US Citizenship?   my responsibilities of US Citizenship.

48. If the law requires it, are you willing to **bear arms** on behalf of the US**?**
What is "to bear arms"?   I will use a weapon to protect the US.

49. Are you willing to perform **noncombatant services** in the US armed forces?
What is "noncombatant"?   To work in the army without using
                                 a gun.

50. Are you willing to perform **work of national importance** under civilian direction**?**
What is a national emergency?   A flood, earthquake, or terrorist attack.
What is work of nat'l importance?   To work on a project for US security.
What is under civilian direction?   To obey non-military safety officers.

The SIMPLIFIED Oath of Allegiance

Write the correct phrase in bold under each picture.

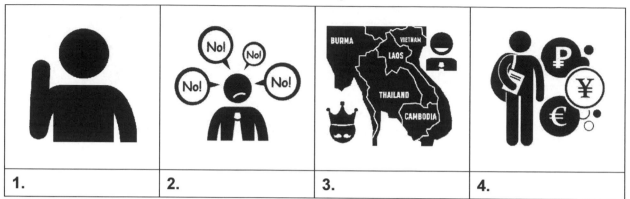

I **promise** that I will **not follow or obey** the **leader of the country** which **I came from**.

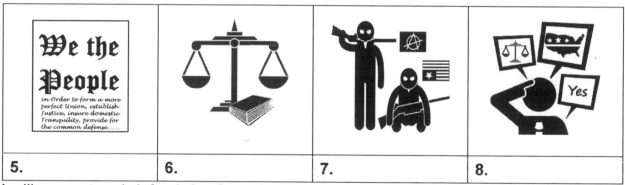

I will support and defend **the Constitution** and **laws of the United States** against **all enemies,** foreign and domestic; I promise to obey the Constitution and be **loyal** to the government of the United States.

If required by law, I will **bear arms** (use a weapon) to protect the United States.
If required by law, I will perform **noncombatant service** (work without using a weapon) in the Armed Forces of the United States.
If required by law, I will help during a national **emergency** or do important work.
I freely take on the **responsibilities of US Citizenship**.

Compare the Oath of Allegiance and the Simplified Oath of Allegiance

	that I absolutely and entirely renounce and abjure all allegiance and fidelity to any foreign prince, potentate, state, or sovereignty of whom or which I have heretofore been a subject or citizen;
		Renounce and abjure	To say "No."	
		Foreign prince, potentate, state, or sovereignty	Leaders of other countries	
	I promise that I will not follow or obey the leader of the country which I came from.
We the People	**that I will support and defend the Constitution and laws of the United States of America against all enemies, foreign and domestic**
		The Constitution	The supreme law of the land	
	I promise to follow the laws of the United States.
	that I will bear true faith and allegiance to the same;
		True faith and allegiance	Loyalty	
	I promise to be loyal to the United States.
	that I will bear arms on behalf of the United States when required by the law;
		Bear arms	To use a weapon to protect the United States	
	I promise to use a weapon to protect the United States if needed.
	that I will perform noncombatant service in the Armed Forces of the United States when required by the law;
		Noncombatant	Work in the army without using a weapon	
	I promise to work in the US armed forces without using a weapon if needed.
	that I will perform work of national importance under civilian direction when required by the law;
		Work of national importance	To do important work (emergency / security)	
	I promise to do important work or help in an emergency if needed.
	and that I take this obligation freely, without any mental reservation or purpose of evasion; so help me God.
		Obligation	Responsibility	
	I freely want to take on the responsibilities of U.S. citizenship.

The Oath of Allegiance

Write the correct word in bold under each picture.

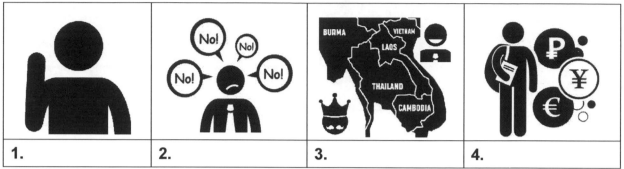

1.   2.   3.   4.

I hereby declare, on **oath**, that I absolutely and entirely **renounce and abjure** all allegiance and fidelity to any **foreign prince, potentate, state, or sovereignty** of whom or which I have heretofore been a **subject or citizen**;

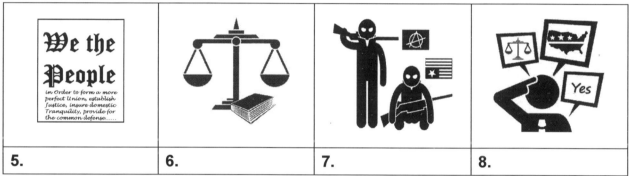

5.   6.   7.   8.

that I will support and defend **the Constitution** and **laws of the United States of America** against **all enemies, foreign and domestic**; that I will bear **true faith and allegiance** to the same;

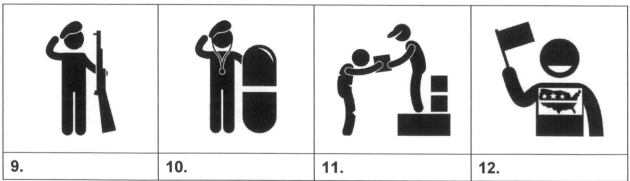

9.   10.   11.   12.

that I will **bear arms** on behalf of the United States when required by the law; that I will perform **noncombatant service** in the Armed Forces of the United States when required by the law; that I will **perform work of national importance under civilian** direction when required by the law; and that **I take this obligation freely**, without any mental reservation or purpose of evasion; so help me God.

Oath of Allegiance Vocabulary Review

Renounce and Abjure
To say "No."

Allegiance and Fidelity
Loyalty (to other countries).

Foreign Prince, Potentate, State, or Sovereignty
Leaders, government, or political parties of other countries.

Heretofore been a Subject or Citizen
My legal status in my previous country of nationality.

Constitution
The supreme law of the United States.

Enemies, Foreign and Domestic
People inside or outside of the United States who want to hurt or destroy America.

True Faith and Allegiance
Loyalty (to the United States).

Bear Arms
To use a weapon to protect the United States.

Noncombatant
To work in the United States armed forces without using a weapon.

Work of National Importance
To do important work for the safety and security of the United States.

Obligation
To take on a responsibility or duty because of a law or moral principle.

Freely
To do something because I want to do it, not because I was forced to do it.

So help me God
I solemnly swear that I will do everything I can to fulfill the responsibilities.

Oath of Allegiance Vocabulary Quiz

Write the vocabulary next to the definition.

- Allegiance and Fidelity
- Bear Arms
- Constitution
- Enemies, Foreign and Domestic
- Foreign Prince, Potentate, State, or Sovereignty
- Freely

- Heretofore been a Subject or Citizen
- Noncombatant
- Obligation
- Renounce and Abjure
- So help me God
- True Faith and Allegiance
- Work of National Importance

1. _____: To say "No."

2. _____: Loyalty (to other countries).

3. _____: Leaders, government, or political parties of other countries.

4. _____: My legal status in my previous country of nationality.

5. _____: The supreme law of the United States.

6. _____: People inside or outside of the United States who want to hurt or destroy America.

7. _____: Loyalty (to the United States).

8. _____: To use a weapon to protect the United States.

9. _____: To work in the US armed forces without using a weapon.

10. _____: To do important work for the safety of the US.

11. _____: To take on a responsibility or duty because of a law or moral principle.

12. _____: To do something because I want to do it, not because I was forced to do it.

13. _____: I solemnly swear that I will do everything I can to fulfill my responsibilities.

Oath of Allegiance Quiz

Circle the correct answer.

1. **When I take the Oath of _____, I promise to be loyal to the US.**
   a. Alienation
   b. Allegiance
   c. Alliance
   d. Armed Forces

2. **"I absolutely and entirely renounce and abjure" means that:**
   a. I am a citizen of my old country and a citizen of the United States.
   b. I am no longer a citizen of my old country. I am only a citizen of the US.
   c. I reject the language and culture of my country of origin.
   d. I want to change my name.

3. **"Foreign Prince, Potentate, State, Sovereignty" are examples of:**
   a. Foreign currency (bills and coins)
   b. Forms of Government
   c. Political Parties
   d. The leaders of my old country

4. **I obey all American laws. I support the _____ because it is the highest law in the United States and is the plan of US government.**
   a. Bill of Rights
   b. Constitution
   c. Oath of Allegiance
   d. Pledge of Allegiance

5. **"I will support the US form of government": _____ (we vote for our leaders) and _____ (we elect representatives to make laws for us).**
   a. democratic and republican
   b. Democratic Party and Republican Party
   c. federal and state
   d. municipal and county

6. **"I will defend the Constitution against all enemies, foreign and domestic" means:**
   a. I will always carry a weapon.
   b. I will follow the laws of the United States.
   c. I will not let anyone hurt the Constitution, the government, or the people.
   d. I will not let anyone say bad things about the US government.

7. **"I will bear true faith and allegiance" means:**
   a. I promise with my life that I will always be loyal to the United States.
   b. I will always vote for the party in power (even if I disagree with the leaders).
   c. I will bear arms when the law does not require me to carry a weapon.
   d. I will pray for the United States.

8. **The US Armed Forces includes:**
   a. The Army, Navy, Air Force, Marines, and National Guard
   b. The Republican and Democratic Parties
   c. The Senate and the House of Representatives
   d. The National Rifle Association

9. **If the US government asks me to _____, I will carry a weapon to protect the country.**
   a. arm our allies
   b. bear arms
   c. perform noncombatant services
   d. play Mortal Kombat

10. **I want to protect the US, but I am afraid of guns. In an emergency, I will work to support the armed forces. I will be:**
    a. a Citizen
    b. a Noncombatant
    c. a Resident
    d. a Soldier

11. **There are many useful jobs that support the armed forces and do not use guns. What noncombatant jobs would help the armed forces?**
    a. "Meth" cook or drug dealer
    b. Human trafficker and arms dealer

   c. Terrorist and neo-fascist party members

   d. Translator and computer programmer

12. **In order to prevent an emergency, I promise to do work of national importance such as:**
   a. I am a computer security expert. I work for a company that stops cyber-attacks.
   b. I am a manicurist. I can paint the presidents on your nails.
   c. I am a Vietnamese pastry chef. I make a really beautiful Jell-O cake.
   d. I am an entrepreneur. I help people start new businesses.

13. **During an emergency, I promise to work under civilian direction. Civilian direction includes:**
   a. The National Guard
   b. The Red Cross, Mayor, and Community leaders
   c. The Sheriff, Police, and Fire Departments
   d. US Armed Forces Officers

14. **"That I take this obligation freely and without any mental reservation" means:**
   a. I have never stayed in a mental hospital.
   b. I make my own decisions. I am not legally incompetent.
   c. I must become an American citizen to stay in the United States.
   d. I want to become an American citizen. No one is forcing me or scaring me into doing it.

15. **"So help me God" means that:**
   a. You can practice any religion or not practice a religion.
   b. I believe in God.
   c. I support freedom of religion.
   d. I will do everything I can to be a good citizen.

Answer Key

Answers to N-400 and Oath of Allegiance Quizzes

Before You Begin: Pictures
1. Age
2. Native Language
3. English Test
4. Civics Test
5. Exemption
6. Disability
7. Impairment
8. Accommodations
9. Interpreter

Before You Begin: Definitions
1, Age
2. Disability
3. Impairment
4. Accommodations
5. Civics Test
6. Native Language
7. English Test
8. Interpreter
9. Exemption

Interview 01: Pictures
1. Name
2. Permanent Resident
3. Citizen
4. Married
5. Month
6. Year
7. The Constitution
8. Vote
9. President

Interview 01: Definitions
1. Year
2. Month
3. The Constitution
4. Vote
5. President
6. Name
7. Married
8. Permanent Resident
9. Citizen

Interview 02: Pictures
1. Date of Birth
2. Country of Birth
3. Address
4. Work
5. Children
6. Arrested
7. Independence Day
8. State Capital
9. US Capital

Interview 02: Definitions
1. Work
2. Country of Birth
3. Date of Birth
4. Children
5. State Capital
6. US Capital
7. Independence Day
8. Address
9. Arrested

Interview 03: Pictures
1. Marital Status
2. Single
3. Widowed
4. Divorced
5. Claim
6. Truth
7. Statue of Liberty
8. Taxes
9. Law

Interview 03: Definitions
1. Statue of Liberty
2. Marital Status
3. Taxes
4. Single
5. Widowed
6. Law
7. Divorced
8. Truth
9. Claim

Interview 04: Pictures
1. Eligibility
2. Residence: 5 years
3. Marriage: 3 years
4. Previous Address
5. Hurt
6. Crime
7. Congress
8. Territory
9. War

Interview 04: Definitions
1. Congress
2. War
3. Territory
4. Eligibility
5. Previous Address
6. Hurt
7. Marriage: 3 years
8. Residence: 5 years
9. Crime

Interview 05: Pictures
1. Green Card
2. Driver's License
3. Legal Name
4. Country of Nationality
5. Travel
6. Form of Government
7. George Washington
8. River
9. Economic System

Interview 05: Definitions
1. Green Card
2. River
3. Legal Name
4. Driver's License
5. Country of Nationality
6. George Washington
7. Form of Government
8. Economic System
9. Travel

Interview 06: Pictures
1. Nobility
2. Terrorist
3. Deported
4. Bear Arms
5. Noncombatant
6. Emergency
7. Senator
8. Amendment
9. Native American

Interview 06: Definitions
1. Emergency
2. Amendment
3. Nobility
4. Terrorist
5. Native American
6. Senator
7. Deported
8. Bear Arms
9. Noncombatant

Interview 07: Pictures
1. Port of Entry
2. Legally Incompetent
3. Communism
4. Habitual Drunkard
5. Illegal Drugs
6. Illegal Gambling
7. Cabinet
8. Declaration of Independence
9. Judicial Branch

Interview 07: Definitions
1. Habitual Drunkard
2. Legally Incompetent
3. Communism
4. Declaration of Independence
5. Illegal Drugs
6. Cabinet
7. Judicial Branch
8. Port of Entry
9. Illegal Gambling

Interview 08: Pictures
1. Financial Support
2. School
3. Retired
4. Spouse
5. Ex-Spouse
6. Work of Nat'l Importance
7. Freedom of Speech
8. Freedom of Religion
9. House of Representatives

Interview 08: Definitions
1. Financial Support
2. Spouse
3. Ex-Spouse
4. House of Representatives
5. Freedom of Speech
6. Work of Nat'l Importance
7. School
8. Retired
9. Freedom of Religion

Interview 09: Pictures
1. Military
2. Rebel
3. Gang
4. Weapons
5. Child Soldier
6. US Armed Forces
7. Life and Liberty
8. Slavery
9. Selective Service

Interview 09: Definitions
1. Child Soldier
2. Rebel
3. Gang
4. Selective Service
5. Weapons
6. Life and Liberty
7. Military
8. US Armed Forces
9. Slavery

Interview 10: Pictures
1. Small Talk
2. Become a US Citizen
3. Miss
4. Persecute
5. Illegal Entry
6. Oath of Allegiance
7. Freedom of the Press
8. Women's Rights
9. Civil Rights

Interview 10: Definitions
1. Small Talk
2. Miss
3. Oath of Allegiance
4. Women's Rights
5. Freedom of the Press
6. Civil Rights
7. Persecute
8. Illegal Entry
9. Become a US Citizen

Oath: USCIS 100:53

1. give up loyalty to other countries
2. defend the Constitution and laws of the United States
3. obey the laws of the US
4. serve in the US military (if needed)
5. serve (do important work for) the nation (if needed)
6. be loyal to the United States

Oath: Simplified

1. promise
2. not follow or obey
3. leader of the country
4. (the country) I came from
5. the Constitution
6. laws of the United States
7. against all enemies
8. loyal
9. bear arms
10. noncombatant service
11. emergency
12. responsibilities of US Citizenship

Oath: N-400 Part 12:45-50

1. US Constitution
2. form of government
3. Oath of Allegiance
4. bear arms
5. noncombatant services
6. work of national importance

Oath of Allegiance

1. oath
2. renounce and abjure
3. foreign prince, potentate, state, or sovereignty
4. subject or citizen
5. the Constitution
6. laws of the United States of America
7. all enemies, foreign and domestic
8. true faith and allegiance
9. bear arms
10. noncombatant service
11. work of national importance
12. I take this obligation freely

Oath of Allegiance Vocabulary Quiz

1. Renounce and Abjure
2. Allegiance and Fidelity
3. Foreign Prince, Potentate, State, or Sovereignty
4. Heretofore been a Subject or Citizen
5. Constitution
6. Enemies, Foreign and Domestic
7. True Faith and Allegiance
8. Bear Arms
9. Noncombatant
10. Work of National Importance
12. Obligation
12, Freely
13. So help me God.

Oath of Allegiance Quiz

1. b. Allegiance
2. b. I am no longer a citizen of my old country. I am only a citizen of the US
3. d. The leaders of my old country.
4. b. The Constitution
5. a. democratic and republican
6. c. I will not let anyone hurt the Constitution, the government, or the people.
7. a. I promise with my life that I will always be loyal to the United States
8. a. The Army, Navy, Air Force, Marines, and National Guard
9. b. bear arms
10. b. a Noncombatant
11. d. Translator and computer programmer
12. a. I am a computer security expert. I work for a company that stops cyber-attacks.
13. b. The Red Cross, Mayor, and Community leaders
14. d. I want to become an American citizen. No one is forcing me or scaring me.
15. d. I will do everything I can to be a good citizen

Section 2

Prepare for the Civics Test

Quiz 01: USCIS 100:01-12
Principles of American Democracy
(circle the correct answer)

---

1. **What is the supreme law of the land?**

   a) The Bill of Rights
   b) The Constitution
   c) The Emancipation Proclamation
   d) The Federalist Papers

2. **What does the Constitution do?**

   a) Sets up the banks
   b) Sets up corporations
   c) Sets up the government
   d) Sets up political parties

3. **The idea of self-government is in the first three words of the Constitution. What are these words?**

   a) E Pluribus Unum
   b) Free the slaves
   c) We the People
   d) Yes, we can!

4. **What is an amendment?**

   a) A change to the Credit Ratings
   b) A change to the Declaration of Independence
   c) A change to the Oath of Allegiance
   d) A change to the US Constitution

5. **What do we call the first ten amendments to the Constitution?**

a) Bill of Rights
b) Civil Rights and Responsibilities
c) Oath of Allegiance
d) Pledge of Allegiance

6. **What is one right or freedom from the First Amendment?**

a) Happiness
b) Jobs
c) Speech
d) Schools

7. **How many amendments does the Constitution have?**

a) 10
b) 18
c) 21
d) 27

8. **What did the Declaration of Independence do?**

a) Announced our independence
b) Elected the first President
c) Freed the slaves
d) Ensured voting rights for all people

9. **What are two rights in the Declaration of Independence?**

a) Liberty, pursuit of happiness
b) Peace, prosperity
c) Property, profits
d) Speech, press

10. What is freedom of religion?

a) You can practice any religion, or not practice a religion.

b) You cannot practice any religion.

c) You must practice a religion.

d) You must practice only one religion.

11. What is the economic system in the United States?

a) Capitalist economy

b) Consumer-centric economy

c) Socialist economy

d) State-planned economy

12. What is the "rule of law"?

a) Adults must obey the law.

b) Employees must obey their supervisors.

c) Government officials are above the law.

d) No one is above the law.

Quiz 02: USCIS 100:13-25
Branches of Government Part 1
(circle the correct answer)

---

13. **Name one branch or part of the government.**

    a) The Department of Homeland Security
    b) The Electoral College
    c) The Federal Reserve Bank
    d) The Legislative Branch

14. **What stops one branch of government from becoming too powerful?**

    a) Balanced budgets
    b) Balanced checkbooks
    c) Checks and balances
    d) Checks and credit cards

15. **Who is in charge of the Executive Branch?**

    a) The Mayor of Washington, DC
    b) The President
    c) The Speaker of the House
    d) The Vice President

16. **Who makes federal laws?**

    a) The Cabinet
    b) The Congress
    c) The President
    d) The Supreme Court

17. What are the two parts of the US Congress?

a) The Army and Navy
b) The Cabinet and Bar
c) The NFL and NBA
d) The Senate and House

18. How many US Senators are there?

a) Twenty-seven (27)
b) Fifty (50)
c) One hundred (100)
d) Four hundred thirty-five (435)

19. We elect a US Senator for how many years?

a) Two (2)
b) Four (4)
c) Six (6)
d) Nine (9)

20. Who is one of your state's current US Senators?

a) Dianne Feinstein
b) Kay Bailey Hutchison
c) Tim Kaine
d) Other _____

21. The House of Representatives has how many voting members?

a) Twenty-one (21)
b) Twenty-seven (27)
c) One hundred (100)
d) Four hundred thirty-five (435)

22. **We elect a US Representative for how many years?**

a) 2 years

b) 4 years

c) 6 years

d) 8 years

23. **Name your US Representative.**

a) Anna Eshoo

b) Ro Khanna

c) Other_____

d) Zoe Lofgren

24. **Who does a US Senator represent?**

a) All adults of the state

b) All citizens of the state

c) All people of the state

d) All voters of the state

25. **Why do some states have more Representatives than other states?**

a) Some states have more cities

b) Some states have more citizens

c) Some states have more people

d) Some states have more votes

Quiz 03: USCIS 100:26-36
Branches of Government Part 2
(circle the correct answer)

26. **We elect a President for how many years?**

    a) 2 years
    b) 4 years
    c) 6 years
    d) 8 years

27. **In what month do we vote for President?**

    a) January
    b) February
    c) October
    d) November

28. **What is the name of the current President of the United States?**

    a) Hillary Clinton
    b) Mike Pence
    c) Paul Ryan
    d) Donald Trump

29. **What is the name of the current Vice President of the United States?**

    a) Al Gore
    b) Mike Pence
    c) Paul Ryan
    d) Tim Kaine

30. **If the President can no longer serve, who becomes President?**

a) First Lady
b) Secretary of State
c) Speaker of the House
d) Vice President

31. **If both the President and the Vice President can no longer serve, who becomes President?**

a) First Lady
b) Secretary of Labor
c) Secretary of State
d) Speaker of the House

32. **Who is the Commander in Chief of the military?**

a) The President
b) The Secretary of Defense
c) The Speaker of the House
d) The Vice President

33. **Who signs bills to become laws?**

a) The President
b) The Secretary of State
c) The Speaker of the House
d) The Vice President

34. **Who vetoes bills?**

a) The President
b) The President Pro Tempore
c) The Speaker of the House
d) The Vice President

35. What does the President's Cabinet do?

a) Advises the President
b) Balances the President
c) Checks the President
d) Vetoes the President

36. What are two Cabinet-level positions?

a) Mayor of Washington, DC
b) Secretary of State
c) Secretary of the Treasury
d) Speaker of the House

Quiz 04: USCIS 100:37-47
Branches of Government Part 3
(circle the correct answer)

37. **What does the judicial branch do?**

    a) Explains laws
    b) Enforces laws
    c) Makes laws
    d) Vetoes laws

38. **What is the highest court in the United States?**

    a) The Department of Justice
    b) The Supreme Court
    c) The Superior Court
    d) The Supreme Law

39. **How many justices are on the Supreme Court?**

    a) Two (2)
    b) Four (4)
    c) Six (6)
    d) Nine (9)

40. **Who is the current Chief Justice of the United States?**

    a) Clarence Thomas
    b) John G. Roberts Jr.
    c) Sandra Day O'Connor
    d) Sonia Sotomayor

41. **Under our Constitution, some powers belong to the federal government. What is one power of the federal government?**

   a) To print licenses
   b) To print money
   c) To provide schools
   d) To provide soldiers

42. **Under our Constitution, some powers belong to the states. What is one power of the states?**

   a) To print licenses
   b) To print money
   c) To provide schools
   d) To provide soldiers

43. **Who is the current Governor of your state?**

   a) Chris Christie
   b) Jerry Brown
   c) Nikki Haley
   d) Other _____

44. **What is the capital of your state?**

   a) Sacramento
   b) Salem
   c) Santa Fe
   d) Other: _____

45. **What are the two major political parties in the United States? (circle 2)**

   a) The Democratic Party
   b) The Green Party
   c) The Libertarian Party
   d) The Republican Party

46. **What is the political party of the current President?**

a) The Democratic Party
b) The Green Party
c) The Libertarian Party
d) The Republican Party

47. **What is the name of the current Speaker of the House of Representatives?**

a) (Dennis) Hastert
b) (John) Boehner
c) (Nancy) Pelosi
d) (Paul) Ryan

Quiz 05: USCIS 100:48-57:
Rights and Responsibilities

(circle the correct answer)

---

48. **There are four amendments to the Constitution about who can vote.**

    a) 16-year-olds and older can vote.
    b) Any permanent resident can vote.
    c) Anyone can vote.
    d) Women and men citizens can vote.

49. **What is one responsibility that is only for United States citizens?**

    a) Serve in a restaurant
    b) Serve in the military
    c) Serve on a committee
    d) Serve on a jury

50. **Name one right only for United States citizens.**

    a) Education at a state school
    b) Vote in a federal election
    c) Vote in a state election
    d) Work for city government

51. **What are two rights of everyone living in the United States? (circle 2)**

    a) Freedom of education
    b) Freedom of expression
    c) Freedom of travel
    d) Freedom of religion

52. What do we show loyalty to when we say the Pledge of Allegiance?

    a)   The party of the President
    b)   The President
    c)   The United States
    d)   Your state's Constitution

53. What is one promise you make when you become a United States citizen?

    a)   To be loyal to the United States
    b)   To join the army
    c)   To speak English only
    d)   To travel inside the United States

54. How old do citizens have to be to vote for President?

    a)   18
    b)   21
    c)   25
    d)   26

55. What are two ways that Americans can participate in their democracy? (pick 2)

    a)   Avoid paying taxes
    b)   Join a civic group
    c)   Play the state lottery
    d)   Vote

56. When is the last day you can send in federal income tax forms?

    a)   January 1
    b)   April 15
    c)   June 30
    d)   December 31

57. **When must all men register for the Selective Service?**

a) 18
b) 21
c) 26
d) 32

Quiz 06: USCIS 100:58-70
Colonial Period and Independence
(circle the correct answer)

---

58. **What is one reason colonists came to America?**

a) Free
b) Free labor
c) Free love
d) Freedom

59. **Who lived in America before the Europeans arrived?**

a) Africans
b) Americans Indians
c) Conquistadores
d) Pilgrims

60. **What group of people was taken to America and sold as slaves?**

a) Africans
b) Americans Indians
c) Conquistadores
d) Pilgrims

61. **Why did the colonists fight the British?**

a) Because of free land
b) Because of high taxes
c) Because of self-government
d) Because of slavery

62. Who wrote the Declaration of Independence?

a) Alexander Hamilton
b) Benjamin Franklin
c) John Adams
d) Thomas Jefferson

63. When was the Declaration of Independence adopted?

a) April 19, 1775
b) July 4, 1776
c) September 17, 1787
d) December 15, 1791

64. There were 13 original states. (Circle 3)

a) Maryland
b) Georgia
c) New Mexico
d) Pennsylvania

65. What happened at the Constitutional Convention?

a) Declaration of Independence was signed.
b) The Bill of Rights was adopted.
c) "The Star-Spangled Banner" was sung.
d) The US Constitution was written.

66. When was the Constitution written?

a) 1776
b) 1787
c) 1789
d) 1791

67. The Federalist Papers supported the passage of the US Constitution. Name one of the writers.

a) Alexander Hamilton
b) Benjamin Franklin
c) George Washington
d) Thomas Paine

68. What is one thing Benjamin Franklin is famous for?

a) He is on the $100 bill
b) Philadelphia newspapers
c) Started the first free libraries
d) Wrote the Declaration of Independence

69. Who is the "Father of Our Country"?

a) Benjamin Franklin
b) George Washington
c) John Adams
d) Thomas Jefferson

70. Who was the first President?

a) Adams
b) Franklin
c) Jefferson
d) Washington

Quiz 07: USCIS 100:71-77
American History: the 1800s
(circle the correct answer)

71. **What territory did the United States buy from France in 1803?**

    a) Florida
    b) Louisiana
    c) Oregon
    d) Texas

72. **Name one war fought by the United States in the 1800s. (Circle 1; 4 are correct)**

    a) Civil War
    b) Mexican-American War
    c) Revolutionary War
    d) Spanish-American War
    e) Vietnam War
    f) War of 1812
    g) World War I
    h) World War II

73. **Name the US war between the North and the South.**

    a) Civil War
    b) Korean War
    c) World War I
    d) War of 1812

74. Name one problem that led to the Civil War.

a) Alcoholism
b) Child labor
c) High taxes
d) Slavery

75. What was one important thing that Abraham Lincoln did?

a) Fought for women's rights
b) Freed the slaves
c) Made the sale of alcohol illegal
d) Supported labor unions

76. What did the Emancipation Proclamation do?

a) Freed the child laborers
b) Freed the servants
c) Freed the slaves
d) Freed the women

77. What did Susan B. Anthony do?

a) Fought against women's rights
b) Fought for women's rights
c) Fought in the Civil War
d) Fought in World War I

Quiz 08: USCIS 100:78-87

Recent American History and Other Important Historical Information

(circle the correct answer)

78. **Name one war fought by the United States in the 1900s. (Circle 1; 5 are correct)**

    a) Civil War
    b) Korean War
    c) Mexican-American War
    d) (Persian) Gulf War
    e) Spanish-American War
    f) Vietnam War
    g) World War I
    h) World War II

79. **Who was President during World War I?**

    a) Thomas Jefferson
    b) Franklin Roosevelt
    c) Theodore Roosevelt
    d) Woodrow Wilson

80. **Who was President during the Great Depression and World War II?**

    a) Dwight D. Eisenhower
    b) Franklin Roosevelt
    c) Theodore Roosevelt
    d) Woodrow Wilson

81. **Who did the United States fight in World War II?**

   a) China, Cuba, N. Korea
   b) England, Scotland, Wales
   c) Japan, Italy, Germany
   d) Poland, Serbia, Russia

82. **Before he was President, Eisenhower was a general. What war was he in?**

   a) Korean War
   b) Spanish-American War
   c) World War I
   d) World War II

83. **During the Cold War, what was the main concern of the United States?**
   a) Communism
   b) Fascism
   c) Fundamentalism
   d) Terrorism

84. **What movement tried to end racial discrimination?**
   a) The Civil Rights Movement
   b) The Feminist Movement
   c) The Peace Movement
   d) The Temperance Movement

85. **What did Martin Luther King Jr. do?**

   a) Fought against civil rights
   b) Fought for civil rights
   c) Fought in WWII
   d) Fought in the Vietnam War

86. **What major event happened on September 11, 2001, in the United States?**

   a) Capitalists attacked Iraq.

   b) Communists attacked Afghanistan.

   c) Fascists attacked Argentina.

   d) Terrorists attacked the United States.

87. **Name one American Indian tribe in the United States.**

   a) Chinese

   b) Chippewa

   c) Costa Rican

   d) Columbian

Quiz 09: USCIS 100:88-95
Integrated Civics: Geography
(circle the correct answer)

---

88. **Name one of the two longest rivers in the United States.**

a) Arkansas

b) Mississippi

c) Rio Grande

d) Snake

89. **What ocean is on the West Coast of the United States?**

a) Atlantic

b) Missouri

c) Mississippi

d) Pacific

90. **What ocean is on the East Coast of the United States?**

a) Atlantic

b) Missouri

c) Mississippi

d) Pacific

91. **Name one US territory.**

a) Alaska

b) Hawaii

c) Puerto Rico

d) Rhode Island

92. **Name one state that borders Canada.**

a) California

b) Florida

c) Iowa

d) Washington

93. Name one state that borders Mexico.

a) California
b) Florida
c) Iowa
d) Washington

94. What is the capital of the United States?

a) Boston
b) New York City
c) Philadelphia
d) Washington, DC

95. Where is the Statue of Liberty?

a) Hudson Bay
b) Manhattan
c) New Jersey Turnpike
d) New York Harbor

Quiz 10: USCIS 100:96-100
Integrated Civics: Symbols and Holidays
(circle the correct answer)

96. **Why does the flag have 13 stripes?**

    a) Because 13 people signed the Constitution.
    b) Because Flag Day is on June 13.
    c) Because there are 13 amendments.
    d) Because there were 13 original colonies.

97. **Why does the flag have 50 stars?**

    a) Because there is one star for each amendment.
    b) Because there is one star for each President.
    c) Because there is one star for each senator.
    d) Because there is one star for each state.

98. **What is the name of the national anthem?**

    a) "The Star-Spangled Banner"
    b) "America, the Beautiful"
    c) "This Land Is Your Land"
    d) "God Bless America"

99. **When do we celebrate Independence Day?**

    a) January 15
    b) April 4
    c) July 4
    d) August 15

100. **Name two national US holidays.**

    a) Bill of Rights Day
    b) Constitution Day
    c) Presidents' Day
    d) Thanksgiving

Answers for Quiz 01: USCIS 100:01-12
Principles of American Democracy

01. B. **The Constitution** is the supreme law of the land.

02. C. The Constitution **sets up the government.**

03. C. **"We the People"** are the first three words of the Constitution.

04. D. An amendment is **a change to the Constitution.**

05. A. **The Bill of Rights** is the first 10 amendments to the Constitution.

06. C. **Speech** is one right or freedom from the First Amendment.

07. D. The Constitution has **twenty-seven (27)** amendments.

08. A. The Declaration of Independence **announced our independence** from Great Britain.

09. A. **Liberty** and **the pursuit of happiness** are two rights in the Declaration of Independence.

10. A. Freedom of religion means **you can practice any religion, or not practice a religion.**

11. A. The United States has a **capitalist economy.**

12. D. The "rule of law" means **no one is above the law.**

Answers for Quiz 02: USCIS 100:13-25
Branches of Government Part 1

13. D. **The Legislative Branch** is one branch or part of the government.

14. C. **Checks and balances** stop one branch of government from becoming too powerful.

15. B. **The President** is in charge of the Executive Branch.

16. B. **Congress** makes federal laws.

17. D. **The Senate and House (of Representatives)** are the two parts of the US Congress.

18. C. There are **one hundred (100)** US Senators.

19. C. We elect a US Senator for **six (6)** years.

20. A. Answers will vary. **Dianne Feinstein** is one of California's US Senators.

21. D. The House of Representatives has **four hundred thirty-five (435)** voting members.

22. A. We elect a US Representative for **two (2)** years.

23. B. Answers will vary. Our US Representative is **Ro Khanna (Milpitas/San Jose)**

24. C. A US Senator represents **all people of the state.**

25. C. Some states have more Representatives than other states **because some states have more people.**

Answers for Quiz 03: USCIS 100:26-36
Branches of Government Part 2

26. B. We elect a President for **four (4)** years.

27. D. We vote for President in **November.**

28. D. **Donald Trump** is the current President of the United States.

29. B. **Mike Pence** is the current Vice President of the United States.

30. D. If the President can no longer serve, **the Vice President** becomes President.

31. D. If both the President and the Vice President can no longer serve, **the Speaker of the House** becomes President.

32. A. **The President** is the Commander in Chief of the military.

33. A. **The President** signs bills to become laws.

34. A. **The President** vetoes bills.

35. A. The President's Cabinet **advises the President.**

36. B, C. The **Secretary of State** and **Secretary of Treasury** are two cabinet-level positions.

Answers for Quiz 04: USCIS 100:37-47
Branches of Government Part 3

37. A. The judicial branch **explains laws.**

38. B. **The Supreme Court** is the highest court in the United States.

39. D. There are **nine (9)** justices on the Supreme Court.

40. B. **John Roberts** is the Chief Justice of the United States.

41. B. Under our Constitution, some powers belong to the federal government. One power of the federal government is **to print money.**

42. C. Under our Constitution, some powers belong to the states. One power of the state is to **provide schooling and education.**

43. B. Answers will vary. **Jerry Brown** is the Governor of California.

44. A. Answers will vary. **Sacramento** is the capital of California.

45. A, D. The **Democratic Party** and **Republican Party** are the two major political parties in the United States.

46. D. The **Republican Party** is the political party of the current President.

47. D. **Paul Ryan** is the current Speaker of the House of Representatives.

Answers for Quiz 05: USCIS 100:48-57
Rights and Responsibilities

48. D. There are four amendments to the Constitution about who can vote. One amendment about voting is that **women and men can vote.**

49. D. One responsibility that is only for United States citizens is to **serve on a jury.**

50. B. One right only for United States citizens is to **vote in a federal election.**

51. B, D. Two rights of everyone living in the United States are **freedom of expression** and **freedom of religion.**

52. C. We show loyalty to **the United States** when we say the Pledge of Allegiance.

53. A. When you become a United States citizen, one **promise** you make is to **be loyal to the United States.**

54. A. Citizens have to be to **eighteen (18) and older** vote for President.

55. B, D Two ways that Americans can **participate** in their democracy are **to join a civic group** and **to vote.**

56. B. **April 15** is the last day you can send in federal income tax forms.

57. A. All men register for the Selective Service **between eighteen (18) and twenty-six (26) years of age.**

Answers for Quiz 06: USCIS 100:58-70
Colonial Period and Independence

58. D. One **reason** colonists came to America was for **freedom.**

59. B. **American Indians** lived in America before the Europeans arrived.

60. A. **Africans** were taken to America and sold as slaves.

61. B. The colonists fought the British **because of high taxes (taxation without representation).**

62. D. **Thomas Jefferson** wrote the Declaration of Independence.

63. B. The Declaration of Independence was adopted on **July 4, 1776.**

64. A, B, D. There were 13 original states. Three states are **Pennsylvania, Maryland, and Georgia.**

65. D. **The Constitution was written** at the Constitutional Convention.

66. B. The Constitution was written in **1787.**

67. A. The Federalist Papers supported the passage of the US Constitution. One of the writers was **Alexander Hamilton**.

68. C. One thing that Benjamin Franklin is famous for is that he **started the first free libraries.**

69. B. The **Father of Our Country** was George Washington.

70. D. **George Washington** was the first President.

Answers for Quiz 07: USCIS 100:71-77
American History: the 1800s

71. B. The United States bought **Louisiana** from France in 1803.

72. There are four possible answers: **Civil War, Mexican-American War, Spanish-American War, War of 1812**

73. A. The US war fought between the North and the South was called the **Civil War.**

74. D. One problem that led to the Civil War was **slavery.**

75. B. Abraham Lincoln **freed the slaves (Emancipation Proclamation).**

76. C. The Emancipation Proclamation **freed the slaves.**

77. A. Susan B. Anthony **fought for women's rights.**

Answers for Quiz 08: USCIS 100:78-87
Recent American History and Other Important Historical Information

78. There are five possible answers: **Korean War, (Persian) Gulf War, Vietnam War, World War I, World War II.**

79. D. **Woodrow Wilson** was the President during World War I.

80. B. **Franklin D. Roosevelt** was the President during the Great Depression and World War II.

81. C. The United States fought **Japan, Germany, and Italy** in World War II.

82. D. Before he was President, Eisenhower was a general. He was in **World War II.**

83. A. During the Cold War, **Communism** was the main concern of the United States.

84. A. The **Civil Rights Movement** tried to end racial discrimination.

85. B. Martin Luther King Jr. **fought for civil rights.**

86. D. **Terrorists attacked the United States** on September 11, 2001 in the United States.

87. B. One American Indian tribe in the United States is the **Chippewa.**

Answers for Quiz 09: USCIS 100:88-95
Integrated Civics: Geography

88. B. One of the two longest rivers in the United States is the **Mississippi River.**

89. D. The **Pacific Ocean** is on the West Coast of the United States.

90. A. The **Atlantic Ocean** is on the East Coast of the United States.

91. C. One US territory is **Puerto Rico.**

92. D. One state that borders Canada is **Washington.**

93. A. One state that borders Mexico is **California.**

94. D. **Washington, D.C.** is the capital of the United States.

95. The Statue of Liberty is in **New York Harbor.**

Answers for Quiz 10: USCIS 100:96-100
Integrated Civics: Symbols and Holidays

96. D. The flag has 13 stripes **because there were 13 original colonies.**

97. D. The flag has 50 stars **because there is one star for each state.**

98. A. **"The Star-Spangled Banner"** is the National Anthem.

99. C. We celebrate Independence Day on **July 4.**

100. C, D. Two national US holidays are **Presidents' Day and Thanksgiving.**

For more Citizenship civics quizzes, go to
http://www.uscitizenpod.com/p/quizzes_06.html

If you need the more answers, go to USCIS Civics Questions and Answers for the
Naturalization Test

Section 3

★ ★ ★

Appendices & Resources

APPENDIX 1: INTERVIEW VOCABULARY REVIEW
(alphabetical order)

Introduction

This glossary contains the N-400 and Civics terms used in this book's Practice Interviews. For more N-400 vocabulary related to the N-400 Part 12, see Appendix 2.

Note to the Reader: During the Citizenship Interview, the USCIS Examiner may ask you to explain some vocabulary. For example, "What is a **habitual drunkard**?" The definitions below are easy and clear responses to such questions.

HINT 1: The Examiner CANNOT explain the question AFTER you've said YES or NO. If you do not fully understand what you are saying, the Examiner will stop the interview.

WRONG:

> Examiner: Have you ever been a **habitual drunkard**?
>
> Applicant: No.
>
> Examiner: What is a **habitual drunkard**?
>
> Applicant: I don't know. . .can you tell me?
>
> Examiner: You promised to tell the truth. You do not understand what you are saying. You do not know if you are saying something that is true or false. We must stop the interview. Go home and study more English.

HINT 2: If an Examiner asks you a question, and you do not understand a word, DO NOT SAY YES OR NO. Ask the examiner to explain the word BEFORE you answer the question.

CORRECT:

> Examiner: Have you ever been a **habitual drunkard**?
>
> Applicant: Excuse me, I don't understand. What is a **habitual drunkard**?
>
> Examiner: A **habitual drunkard** drinks too much alcohol every day and gets sick. A **habitual drunkard** is addicted to alcohol.
>
> Applicant: I understand. No, I have never been a **habitual drunkard**.
>
> Examiner: Let's continue the interview.

N-400 AND CIVICS TERMS USED IN THIS BOOK'S PRACTICE INTERVIEWS

Accommodations

In order to guarantee fair access during the Citizenship interview, USCIS makes small changes to the interview for some older, longtime residents and disabled people.

Address

Location information about the place where a person lives or works.

Age

The year you were born.

Allegiance

Allegiance is loyalty (or to be loyal).

Amendment

A change or addition to the Constitution.

Arrested

To break the law and go to jail.

Bear Arms

Bear arms is to use a weapon to protect the country.

Become a US Citizen

The reason you want to change your Citizenship.

Cabinet

The group of federal department leaders (secretaries) that advise the President.

Citizen

A person who was born in a country or became a member through the law (naturalization).

Child

My son, daughter, or a dependent that I adopted before his or her 18th birthday.

Child Soldier

A child soldier is a child under 15 years old who fights in a militia, army, or rebel group.

Civics Test

I must answer six out of 10 of the USCIS 100 History and Government questions correctly to pass the test.

Civil Rights

The rights that every person should have, such as the right to vote or to be treated fairly by the law.

Claim

To lie or say something false, which is not supported by facts.

Communism

A government with a state-planned economy such as China, Vietnam, North Korea, and Cuba.

Congress

Also known as the Legislative Branch. It is the part of the US government that makes federal laws.

Country of Birth

The country where I was born.

Country of Nationality

The country of which I am currently a citizen.

Crime

To break the law.

Current Home Address

The place where I live now.

Date of Birth

The date when I was born: month / day / year/

Date of Permanent Residence

Date of residence as stated on my Legal Permanent Residence Card.

Declaration of Independence

The announcement that said that the US is a free country.

Deported

Deported is to be arrested and sent back to my old country.

Disability

A problem that stops a person from moving or understanding.

Divorced

The marital status of the people who legally end a marriage.

Driver's License

State-issued identification which permits me to drive.

Economic system

The way a country makes, manages, and spends money.

Eligible or Eligibility

Eligibility is when the law says you can do something. A person is eligible to become a US citizen if they have met age and residence requirements.

Emergency

A big problem that can hurt or kill many people, such as an earthquake, flood, or tornado.

English Test

The questions that the USCIS officer asks me during my interview about my N-400.

Ex-Spouse

My previous husband or wife.

Exemption
In order to guarantee fair access during the Citizenship interview, older longtime residents do not have to do the interview in English (check the requirements).

Financial Support
How I pay for my living expenses such as food and rent.

Foreign Prince, Potentate, State, or Sovereignty
Leaders of other countries. The leader of the country which I came from.

Form of Government
The system of government.

Freedom of Religion
We can practice any religion or not practice a religion

Freedom of Speech
The right to say what we think.

Freedom of the Press
People are free to write and publish what they want.

Gang
A group that uses violence against people.

Green Card
A common name for the Legal Permanent Resident Card. It is a photo identification that says I can legally live and work in the United States.

Habitual Drunkard
A habitual drunkard drinks too much alcohol every day and gets sick. A habitual drunkard is addicted to alcohol.

House of Representatives
The lower house of the US Congress.

Hurt or Kill on Purpose

When a person plans to injure or kill a person and then does it.

Illegal Drugs

Drugs that are against the law.

Illegal Entry

To help others come into the United States without a proper visa, or to stay in the US on an expired visa.

Illegal Gambling

To play cards or games for money and not pay taxes.

Impairment

A body part or bodily sense that is physically or mentally weak.

Income Tax

Income tax is to pay money to the government based on what I earn.

Independence Day

The day every year on which the United States celebrates its freedom from Great Britain (July 4, 1776).

Interpreter

The person who tells another person what someone else says in a different language.

Judicial Branch

The part of government that reviews and explains laws.

Law

The system of rules that the people must follow.

Legal Name

Full name used on legal documents: first name / middle name / last name.

Legally incompetent

I am too sick to make my own decisions. A judge says that a legal guardian such as a family member, doctor, or lawyer, must make decisions for me.

Life and Liberty

To live and be free.

Marital Status

My current marital status: single (never married), married, widowed, or divorced.

Married

To be someone's husband or wife according to the law.

Military Training

A person learns how to use a weapon in the national armed forces to protect the country.

Military

The official armed forces of the national government that protects the country.

Miss

To feel sad because someone or something that you love is not with you.

Month

One of the 12 parts of the year. Most months have 30 or 31 days. February has 28 (or 29) days.

N-400

The USCIS Application for Naturalization. This is the form I use to apply for US Citizenship.

Name

The words people use to identify me, call me, or talk about me.

Native American (American Indian)

The people who are the original residents of the Americas.

Native Language
The language that I spoke in my home country.

Nobility
Nobility is to be a member of the family of a king or queen.

Noncombatant
Noncombatant is to work in the army without using weapons.

Oath
A promise.

Oath of Allegiance
A solemn promise that I will be loyal to the United States. To swear loyalty to the US

Obligation
Responsibility or duty.

Paramilitary Unit
A paramilitary unit is a group of people who act like the military, but are not a part of the official armed forces of the national government.

Permanent Resident
A person who is not a US citizen that the US government says can live in the United States.

Persecute
Persecute is to hate and hurt someone because he or she belongs to a different race, religion, group, gender, sexual orientation, or political party, etc.

President
The leader of the United States. The leader of the Executive Branch which enforces the law.

Previous Address
The place where you lived before your current home.

Port of Entry

My port of entry is the airport or border crossing where I can legally enter a country.

Previous Home Address

The place where you lived before your present address.

Prison camp

Prisoners must work or they are killed or tortured.

Rebel

A group that uses weapons to fight against the government.

Retired

To leave a job and not work anymore.

River

A large body of water that flows across a country.

Selective Service (a.k.a. "Draft")

All male US citizens and male immigrants living in the United States who are age 18 through 25 must register with the Selective Service (sss.gov). These young men will be called to join the armed forces if there is a national emergency.

Senator

A person who represents a state in the US Senate.

School

To go to a college, university, or training program full-time.

Single

The marital status of the person who has never been married.

Slavery

To buy, sell, and own people. To take away a person's rights and force them to work without pay.

Small Talk

Polite, friendly conversation about unimportant topics.

Spouse

My current husband or wife.

State Capital

The city where a state's government meets.

Statue of Liberty

An important symbol of freedom. It is on Liberty Island in New York Harbor.

Taxes

Money to pay for the government, military, healthcare, schools, etc.

Territory

Land that is owned or controlled by a federal government.

Terrorism

People who use violence to destroy governments.

Travel

To go outside of the United States for more than 24 hours.

Truth

To say something true and is supported by facts.

US Armed Forces

To be a member of the United States Army, Navy, Air Force, Marines, or Coast Guard.

US Capital

The city where the federal government meets.

US Constitution

The Constitution is the supreme law of the land.

US Form of Government
The US has a democratic form of government.

Vote
A citizen chooses a new leader or law.

War
Armies fight against each other.

Washington (George Washington)
The first President of the United States.

Weapon
An object that can hurt or kill people or property.

Widowed
The marital status of the spouse who is still alive after the other spouse dies.

Women's Rights
Equal access to schools, jobs, and government services to correct discrimination based on gender (bias against women).

Work
A job that I am paid to do.

Work of National Importance under Civilian Direction
To do work to support our nation's safety and security under the supervision of non-military leaders

Year
365 days or 12 months.

For more vocabulary, go to **Appendix 2: N-400 Part 12 Vocabulary**.

APPENDIX 2: N-400 PART 12 VOCABULARY REVIEW

Introduction

This glossary contains the many of the USCIS N-400 terms in Part 12. Some of these terms have been discussed in the book, and they are included here for further independent practice. They are presented in the order that they appear on the N-400.

Note to the Reader: During the Citizenship Interview, the USCIS Examiner may ask you to explain some vocabulary. For example, "What is **claim**?" The definitions below are easy and clear responses to such questions.

HINT 1: The Examiner CANNOT explain the question AFTER you've said YES or NO. If you do not fully understand what you are saying, the Examiner will stop the interview.

WRONG:

> Examiner: Have you ever **claimed** to be a US citizen?
>
> Applicant: No.
>
> Examiner: What is **claim**?
>
> Applicant: I don't know. . .can you tell me?
>
> Examiner: You promised to tell the truth. You do not understand what you are saying. You do not know if you are saying something that is true or false. We must stop the interview. Go home and study more English.

HINT 2: If an Examiner asks you a question, and you do not understand a word, DO NOT SAY YES OR NO. Ask the examiner to explain the word BEFORE you answer the question.

CORRECT:

> Examiner: Have you ever **claimed** to be a US citizen?
>
> Applicant: Excuse me, I don't understand. What is **claim**?
>
> Examiner: **Claim** is to say something is true even though it is false. Have you ever said that you were a US citizen even though you are not a US citizen?
>
> Applicant: I understand. No, I have never **claimed** to be a US citizen.
>
> Examiner: Let's continue the interview.

N-400 Part 12 Vocabulary Review

Part 12 Questions 1-8

Claim
To say something is true even though it is false.

Register
To put my name and personal information on an official list of people who can vote.

Vote
To choose a new leader or law.

Election
To choose a new leader for a government office.

Nobility
To be a member of the king's (royal) family.

Title of Nobility
A special name or rank.

Legally Incompetent
A judge says that I cannot make important life decisions. A lawyer, doctor, or my family must make decisions for me.

Owe
I must pay the government money.

Taxes
Money for the government. The government uses tax money to pay for the government, military, healthcare, schools, etc.

Non-resident
A "non-resident" does not live in the United States.

Part 12 Detailed Review Questions 9-13 — Affiliations

Group or Organization
People (members) who come together to do something.

Communism
Communism is the government party of China, Vietnam, North Korea, and Cuba.

Totalitarian party
A totalitarian party has complete control over everything and the people have no power.

Terrorist
A terrorist uses violence to control people and governments, ex. September 11, 2001.

Rebel
To advocate the overthrow of any government by either force or violence

Insurgent
To use weapons to fight against the government

Nazi Government
The Nationalist Socialist political party led by Adolf Hitler that controlled Germany from 1933 to 1945

Persecute
To hate or hurt someone who is different from you.

Part 12 Detailed Review Question 14 — Act of Violence

Genocide
Genocide is to kill a group of people because of their race, ethnicity, religion, or gender.

Torture
Torture is to hurt a person so that he or she will tell you secrets or information.

Kill

To kill someone is to cause a person to die; to kill or hurt a person on purpose.

Rape (sexual assault)

Rape is to force a person to have sex.

Religion

Religion is how people worship God.

Part 12 Detailed Review Question 15 — Group Violence

Military Unit

The official armed forces group of the national government that protects the country.

Paramilitary Unit

A group of people who act like the military, but are not a part of the official military.

Police Unit

An official local group that enforces the law, protects people, and stops crime.

Self-Defense Unit

A group of people organized to protect their community against crime and violence

Vigilante Unit

A vigilante unit is a group of people who act like the police, but are not a part of the official police.

Rebel Group

A group fights against the national government.

Guerilla Group

A group is a group of people who use weapons against or otherwise physically attack the military, police, government, or other people.

Militia

An army of people, not part of the official military.

Insurgent Organization

A group that uses weapons and fights against the government.

Part 12 Detailed Review Question 16 — Work in a Prison

Prison or Jail

A place where people who have been charged with a crime are kept.

Prison Camp

A place where enemy prisoners of war are kept.

Detention Facility

A place where people are forced to stay temporarily until they are moved to a prison, labor camp, or are deported.

Labor Camp

A place where people are forced to work.

Part 12 Detailed Review Questions 17-21 — Gang, Weapons, Child Soldiers

Gang

A part of any group that uses a weapon against another person.

Weapon

An object such as a gun, knife, or bomb which can hurt or kill people or property

Threaten

To say that you will hurt or kill a person if they don't do what you tell them to do.

Military or Weapons Training

A person learns how to use a weapon in the armed forces or in a militia.

Recruit

To find new people to join the armed forces.

Enlist

To join the armed forces.

Conscript

To force a person to join the armed forces against his or her will.

Child Soldier

A child under 15 years old who fights in the armed forces.

Part 12 Detailed Review Questions 22-29 — Criminal Records

Crime

To do something illegal or break the law.

Criminal Record

Information kept by the local police or government agency that shows that a person has committed a crime.

Arrested

To break the law and go to jail.

Cited

An official order for someone to appear in court or pay a fine for doing something illegal.

Detained

To be stopped and questioned by the police or government officials.

Charged

The police, judge, or court says that you have broken the law.

Convicted

A judge or court proves that you have committed a crime and must serve time in jail or pay a penalty.

Rehabilitation ("rehab")

A court-ordered program to cure drug or alcohol problems of addiction.

Probation

A period of time during which a criminal is allowed to stay out of prison if that person behaves well, and does not commit another crime.

Jail

People go to jail when they break the law and cannot leave until a judge says that they are free.

Part 12 Detailed Review Question 30 — Crime

Habitual Drunkard

A habitual drunkard drinks too much alcohol every day and gets sick.

Prostitute

A prostitute sells sex. A "john" solicits or "buys" a prostitute's services (including sex).

Illegal drugs

Drugs that are against the law, such as heroin, opium, and cocaine.

Bigamy

To be married to more than one person at the same time.

Immigration Benefit

A person can become eligible for a Legal Permanent Resident status by marrying a US citizen.

Illegal Entry

To come into the United States without a proper visa, or to stay in the US on an expired visa.

Illegal Gambling

To play cards or games for money. It is illegal to gamble and not pay taxes.

Alimony

Money that a court orders someone to pay monthly to their ex-spouse after a divorce.

Public Benefits
Social services or financial support from the government.

Part 12 Detailed Review Questions 31-36 — Deportation

False, Fraudulent, or Misleading
To say or do something that is false or obscures the truth.

Lie
To say something that is not true.

Gain Entry or Admission
To come into the United States.

Gain Immigration Benefits
To get legal residence in the United States.

Remove (removal)
To make someone leave the United States.

Exclude (exclusion)
Not to allow an individual to enter the United States.

Deport (deportation)
To arrest, then force a person to return to the country they came from because they do not have a legal right to stay in the United States.

Ordered
A judge or Immigration officer makes a legal decision that someone must do something.

Rescission (rescind)
The government cancels a person's legal status to enter or live in the US after permission had been originally given.

Proceedings
A legal case to decide a person's immigration status.

Part 12 Detailed Review Questions 37-44 — US Military Service

US Armed Forces
To be a member of the United States Army, Navy, Air Force, Marines, or Coast Guard.

Deployed
To serve (or to be stationed) in the US military service outside of the United States.

Court-martialed
To be arrested and put on trial in a military court.

Discharge
To leave the armed forces.

The Draft
Compulsory military service.

Deserted
To run away from the military service.

Selective Service
All male US citizens and male immigrants living in the United States who are age 18 through 25 must register with the Selective Service (sss.gov). These young men will be called to join the armed forces if there is a national emergency.

Part 12 Detailed Review Questions 45-50 — Attachment to the US Constitution

US Constitution
The supreme law of the United States.

US Form of Government
The United States has a democratic form of government.

Oath
A serious promise.

Allegiance

To be loyal.

The Oath of Allegiance

I promise to be loyal to the United States.

Bear Arms

To use a weapon to protect the United States.

Noncombatant

To work in the army without using a weapon.

Work of National Importance

A major community emergency; example: flood, fire, earthquake.

Under Civilian Direction

To follow the orders of non-military safety officers or disaster relief workers from the Red Cross.

APPENDIX 3: INTERNET CITIZENSHIP RESOURCES

US CITIZENSHIP AND IMMIGRATION SERVICE AND PARTNERS (10 quick links!)

- **USCIS.gov:** The Official Website of the Department of Homeland Security
  - https://www.uscis.gov/
- **USCIS.gov/es:** Sitio web oficial del Departamento de Seguridad Nacional
  - https://www.uscis.gov/es
- **USCIS:** N-400 Application for Naturalization
  - https://www.uscis.gov/n-400
- **USCIS Citizenship Resource Center**: Educational Tools for Citizenship Prep
  - https://www.uscis.gov/citizenship
- **USCIS Multilingual Resources**: USCIS Resources in 26 languages
  - https://www.uscis.gov/tools/multilingual-resource-center
- **USCIS Civics Playlist**: one video for each 100 Civics question
  - https://www.youtube.com/playlist?list=PLpNZsaiyFfG0mZUx6aS8Tn2pAN NymRDaJ
- **myUSCIS:** a new service that helps you navigate the immigration process.
  - https://my.uscis.gov/
- **FTC: Avoiding Scams Against Immigrants**—FTC/USCIS info in 7 languages
  - https://www.consumer.ftc.gov/features/feature-0012-scams-against-immigrants
- **si.edu: Preparing the Oath:** A joint resource of the Smithsonian and the USCIS. A collection of videos and quizzes for each one of the 100 question
  - http://americanhistory.si.edu/citizenship/
- **USCIS** and **USCIS Español** on Facebook, Twitter, Instagram, and **YouTube.**

ESL, CITIZENSHIP, CIVICS, and HISTORY RESOURCES

American English at State: About the USA.

http://americanenglish.state.gov/resources/about-usa

About the USA. examines the customs, government, and history of the United States.

Ben's Guide to the US Government

http://bensguide.gpo.gov/

Ben's Guide is designed to talk about the Federal Government. Check out the Master level Learning Adventures.

CCSF: Best, OK, and Worst Citizenship Interview Strategies

https://www.youtube.com/user/CCSFCITIZENSHIP/videos

50+ videos of mock interviews and interview strategies.

CDLP: Adult Learning Activities: Law and Government

http://www.cdlponline.org/index.cfm?fuseaction=stories&topicID=2

Read and listen to short stories about law and government based on the news.

CitizenshipWorks

https://www.citizenshipworks.org/

This website will help you to understand the naturalization process and prepare for the naturalization tests. Info in 中文, Tiếng Việt, Español, and English, plus free Mobile apps!

CLINIC: The Citizenship Test Guide

https://cliniclegal.org/citizenshiptest

Free downloadable Citizenship Guide and audio file.

CLINIC: "Miguel's Naturalization Interview"

https://cliniclegal.org/sites/default/files/toolkits/citizenship/CLINIC-Graphic-Novel.pdf

Free downloadable graphic novel about a Citizenship interview.

CLINIC: Citizenship for Refugee Elders

https://cliniclegal.org/sites/default/files/citizenship_for_elders_2nd_edition_final.pdf

This handbook contains information on how to create and maintain a citizenship program for older refugee immigrants.

ELCivics.com: Civics Lessons and EL Civics for ESL Students

http://www.elcivics.com/

Learn Civics and ESL with pictures and easy words.

Elizabeth Claire's Easy English News: US Constitution in Simple English

http://www.elizabethclaire.com/products/us-constitution-in-simple-english

A free pdf of the US Constitution with a side-by-side translation in simple English

HIAS: Citizenship Prep Materials

http://www.hias.org/citizenship-prep-materials

Study guides for the US Citizenship test are available in six languages: Arabic, Nepali, Serbo-Croatian/Bosnian, Somali, Spanish, and Vietnamese.

iCivics: Free Lesson Plans and Games for Learning Civics

https://www.icivics.org/

Web-based education project designed to teach students civics and inspire them to be active participants in US democracy. Founded by Justice Sandra Day O'Connor.

ILRC: Annotated N-400 and Translations in Spanish and Other Languages

https://www.ilrc.org/n-400-translations-spanish-other-languages

This is an outstanding collection translations of the N-400 by ILRC and partners.

Jones Library Citizenship Resources

http://www.joneslibrary.org/257/Study-Guides

Check out the Jones Library free, downloadable Citizenship Guide (pdf and audio).

Julie Pittman: USCIS N-400 Naturalization Practice Video Playlist

https://www.youtube.com/playlist?list=PLN59NIDAAhOQHnRah2VbegdIAgCUk5g1N

9 videos review the 2016 N-400 section by section. Good Job, Julie Pittman!

Lessons on American Presidents

http://www.lessonsonamericanpresidents.com/

Handouts, MP3s & Online Quizzes about all 44 US Presidents, by Sean Banville

Listen and Read Along: US Citizenship Test Material

https://www.youtube.com/playlist?list=PL5Zc8v096OOnT0ZSHifhRpnJKbWJECD4-

As the announcer reads the USCIS Study Booklet: "Learn About the United States Quick Civics Lessons" (M-638), the words are highlighted!

USA Learns

http://www.usalearns.org/

USA Learns is a free website to help adults learn English online. Look for their Citizenship Preparation course in late 2017!

US Citizenship Podcast

http://www.uscitizenpod.com/

A daily blog of Citizenship resources (in English and other languages) hosted by Jennifer Gagliardi, the author of *US Citizenship Bootcamp*.

VOA Learning English

http://learningenglish.voanews.com/

Stories and multi-media resources to learn about America and American English.

Find more at http://www.uscitizenpod.com/p/citizenship-resources.html

Acknowledgments

Thanks to the students and staff of **Milpitas Adult School** (adulted.musd.org). I deeply appreciate your enthusiasm, patience, and assistance in developing new Citizenship materials.

Thanks to the **Outreach and Technical Assistance Network** (OTAN.us) for their ongoing leadership to integrate technology's best practices in the adult education classroom and beyond. I, my fellow teachers, and our students have greatly benefited from your technical expertise, passionate commitment to digital literacy, and ongoing friendship.

Thanks to the **Comprehensive Adult Student Assessment Systems** (CASAS.org) for their language and skills assessments. Yes, it's time to take a CASAS test!

Thanks to the **California Adult Literacy Professional Development Project** (CALPRO-online.org) for providing opportunities for professional development for adult education teachers.

Thanks to the **Commission on Adult Basic Education** (COABE.org) and the **California Council for Adult Education** (CCAEstate.org) for representing the needs and interests of the adult education community in Washington, D.C., Sacramento, and beyond.

Thanks to the students and staff of the **Santa Clara County Library District** (sccl.org), **IRC International Rescue** Committee (rescue.org), and **SIREN Services, Immigrant rights and Education Network** (siren-bayarea.org) for their support of the SCCL Citizenship Action Project 2015-2016.

Thanks to **USCIS**, especially Dr. Michael Jones and his staff, SF/SJ officers Rosemary Lucee Fan, Nina Sachdev, and Rebecca Sagun, and the entire USCIS IT team--y'all are delivering on *The Promise that is America!*

Last but not least, thanks to **Lori Saltis** for her love and encouragement in all my endeavors, literary and otherwise. Best.Friend.EVER!

About the Author

Jennifer Gagliardi has been teaching ESL/Citizenship at Milpitas Adult School since 2002. In 2007, she launched US Citizenship Podcast, which distributes Citizenship resources and reports on Citizenship and immigration news. In early 2016, she released the US Citizenship Podcast app on iPhone/iPad and Android. Jennifer is always looking for new ways to help students learn English and Civics so that we can live the American Dream together!

If you have any questions or comments, please visit
- Webpage: http://www.uscitizenpod.com/
- Podcast Webpage: http://uscitizenpod.libsyn.com/
- Email: uscitizenpod@gmail.com
- Facebook: https://www.facebook.com/US-Citizenship-Podcast-369726739857/
- Instagram: https://www.instagram.com/uscitizenpod/
- LearningChocolate: www.learningchocolate.com/users/uscitizenpod/authored
- Twitter: https://twitter.com/uscitizenpod
- YouTube: https://www.youtube.com/user/uscitizenpod
- rss: http://uscitizenpod.libsyn.com/rss

Download the free US Citizenship Podcast app:
- App for iPhone/iPad: https://goo.gl/dLiOAE
- App for Android: https://goo.gl/d6rs9f
- Subscribe to **US Citizenship Podcast** via iTunes: https://goo.gl/BVrqHQ

Good Luck! I know that you will be a great American Citizen!

Also by ESL Publishing

She Built Ships During World War II is a historical novel for English language learners at the intermediate level. It is an excellent way for a student to learn history and English at the same time. The novel can stand alone, or be used in conjunction with the companion workbook (published separately), which is designed for use along with the novel in language classes. The workbook has a rich variety of vocabulary, word-building, and comprehension exercises, as well as writing, discussion, and critical-thinking topics for use in the language classroom.

With meticulous research on the WWII era, Slone weaves an intricate story of cruelty, compassion, and love, reminding us of the injustice of the internment of Japanese Americans and racial prejudice in the armed forces. The courage of women welders who built ships while their husbands were at war is depicted so well that the characters come to life. We watch the heroine, Lolly, struggle to keep her family together while she works as a welder and her husband is away. A tender romance is threaded throughout the book, and we agonize with her as she brings it to an inevitable conclusion. Between the fascinating and sometimes little-known historical facts, and the larger-than-life sympathetic characters, the book is a page-turner to the very end.
Alla Crone, author of *Winds Over Manchuria, East Lies the Sun*, and *Russian Bride*

This workbook is designed to be used in combination with the novel, *She Built Ships During World War II*, in language classes or self-study. Intended to build vocabulary at the intermediate level, it has a variety of words, phrases, and idioms, word-building, structure, and reading comprehension exercises. In addition, it includes writing, discussion, and critical-thinking topics designed for use in the language or reading classroom.

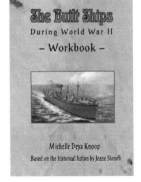

Highlights:

- Vocabulary and idioms are presented and practiced in the context of the novel's storyline.
- Word form and structure exercises support and develop the new vocabulary.
- Critical thinking, writing, and pair/group discussion topics inspire readers to explore the social, personal, ethical, and moral issues raised in the novel.

These two books can be ordered online with a discount for bulk orders.

www.eslpublishing.com

Coming Soon from ESL Publishing

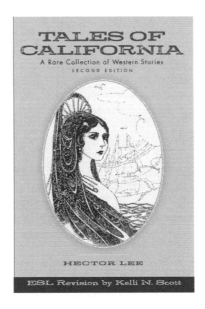

An entertaining book that will allow ESL students to learn and enjoy Western folktales as well as English. Rewritten by an ESL teacher, the original storybook will have a companion workbook.

Available soon on our website!

www.eslpublishing.com

Made in the USA
San Bernardino, CA
14 August 2017